REDEFINING
GENEROSITY

REDEFINING
GENEROSITY

How to Unleash Your Potential
Discover Your Purpose
& Cultivate Connection

BY JAYSON LINFORD

PUBLISHED BY
THE EMPOWERED LIFE PROJECT INTERNATIONAL INC.

REDEFINING GENEROSITY
Copyright © 2017
Jayson Linford

All rights reserved. No part of this publication may be reproduced, stored in a retrieval system, or transmitted in any form or by any means electronic, mechanical, photocopying, recording, or otherwise without prior written permission of the publisher and copyright owner.

Published by The Empowered Life Project International Inc.

Printed in the United States of America.

ISBN-13: 978-0-9995974-0-8

Don't be so attached to the outcome that you miss the magic that happens right in the middle of the journey.

Acknowledgements

Thank you,

To my editors Carrie Snider and Krista Walsh.

To my best friend and wife Brigitte for her support, encouragement, and example.

To my kids Mack, Andi, and Phoebe for their unceasing examples of generosity.

To the people of Ghana I had the privilege of meeting, who were a large inspiration for this book.

To all the people who have allowed me to involve them in this project and have helped carry it forward.

Table of Contents

Introduction 1

Chapter 1: What is Generosity? 7

Chapter 2: Gratitude First 25

Chapter 3: A Generous Disposition 57

Chapter 4: Cognitive Dissonance 81

Chapter 5: The Pity Trap 99

Chapter 6: The Perfect Lie 115

Chapter 7: Intention 137

Chapter 8: Generosity is in Our DNA 157

Chapter 9: Before You Begin Your Experiment 175

Chapter 10: Starting YOUR Generosity Experiment. 191

Conclusion 203

About the Author 205

Introduction

In the fall of 2015, I returned home from a trip I had looked forward to for a long time—a ten-day humanitarian trip to Ghana. I had the opportunity to be immersed in the culture of a small village in Ghana called Jasikan. My time was spent among the locals building homes, playing games, visiting schools, and learning from a different way of life. It didn't take me very long, after I was back home in my routine, to realize that however generous I was, or I thought I was, I had a long way to go to be as generous as I could be. I became keenly aware that I was not as generous as I had previously thought. Sure, I had spent time on a service trip in Ghana. That's pretty generous, right?

Most of us are generous—to a point, but we cannot improve that which we are not aware of. Most of us have a favorable view of how generous we are. We know we could do better, but for the most part we are satisfied. When what we do and how we view ourselves has become part of our routine, it is easy to miss opportunities to not only be more generous but to improve our lives by being more generous.

I have been taught my whole life, as many of us have, about how generosity can increase the feelings of belonging, help you feel more connected, play a part in overall fulfillment, and all the while increasing the joy of the people around you. But I was not giving generosity the effort that was required to acquire the blessings that it had in store for me.—the blessings we all deserve if we will do the work.

With my recent trip to Ghana on my mind, and especially as I dwelled on generosity, I became more aware of generous opportunities that before I would not have seen. It was like putting on glasses for the first time. It was shocking to see myself as I was in comparison to how I thought I was.

I decided to change that, I decided to conduct my own personal Generosity Experiment. For twenty-one days, I focused on developing the habit of being as generous as possible. In just three weeks, I retrained my brain and heart to allow generosity to take full effect in my life.

Going on this journey both excited and scared me. I knew I would have to move out of my comfort zone, I would have opportunities I could never have imagined, and I would have to come to terms with the person I saw in the mirror and make a choice to stay the same or become a different person.

As you will see throughout the chapters of this book, being a more generous person was the goal. That is, my focus was always on generosity. However, there were other principles I discovered along the way, those that were essential not just to living more generously but to living more fully.

We will explore each principle together as we journey through life's situations and circumstances. The principles will empower you to let go of the artificial limitations we unwittingly allow to be placed on us.

This experiment changed my life, and it can do the same for you.

In just twenty-one days, I learned a lot about myself and what generosity really means. I had not realized how accustomed I had become to saying no, and how neatly I had rationalized my life when it came to generosity.

This book will help you to realize what thought processes that need to be let go, it is about creating new habits—ones that would not only empower those around you but that would allow you to live out the full measure of at least this one virtue.

In the end, embracing the true meaning of generosity is the key to living an abundant life.

In psychology there are generally four stages of learning and If you are like I was before my experiment (and I think most everyone is), then you have your butt firmly planted somewhere between the first two levels "unconscious incompetence"—*where you don't know what you don't know*—and "conscious incompetence"—*where you become conscious that you don't know something.* This is where I was with generosity, I was going through the motions and doing what I thought was expected of me.

But even once the third level of learning is reached, a state of conscious competence, where you know what you are missing and you're working towards improvement but your actions still require thought, the work isn't done yet. The problem is that typically when we go to work, we use tactics that only give short-term results. We feel pretty good about this because we are seeing changes...for the time being. But in fact, this will rob you of the long-term satisfaction that comes when you follow the principles you will discover in this book.

Many of us are employing methods and practices that are unintentional. We model certain behaviours because that is what we think is expected of us. These are mostly habits we developed as children and adolescents and others we picked up as a result of our insecurities. When we let our insecurities dictate how we give or receive generosity, our focus is on ourself. When we give to be seen a certain way, or to hide something we don't like in ourselves, we reduce generosity to an impotent virtue.

These practices probably served us at one time, and they are still getting us results in some form today or we would not still be using them. Although, I would venture to say they are not getting you the results that you deserve.

My goal for you in reading this book is the same goal I had for myself—to change, and to achieve "unconscious competence." This is the level where you have had so much practice at doing something that not only do you understand the concept, but it becomes the way you react unconsciously, it becomes part of you. It may take you longer than twenty-one days to achieve this level of learning, but it is well worth it.

In this book, I want to share with you some of my biggest challenges and take-aways as I took this journey, including:

- The core truth of generosity.
- Common misconceptions about generosity.
- Behaviors and thoughts that keep us from being generous.
- The rules of generosity.
- The impact of generosity on others and YOU.

But, keep in mind that you can't read this book for someone else—that would be doing yourself a disservice. Read it for you. Read it with an open heart and with the commitment to question *your own virtue*. Be willing to accept that you may not be as generous as you think you are.

My hope is for all of us to overcome and dismantle the obstacles that prevent us from achieving the pinnacle of this human experience. If all this book does is make facing those stumbling blocks a little easier, then it will have done its job.

Now, I have a higher goal for you as well: I want you to thrive and see each moment as one with great purpose and opportunity. I want you to see the relationships you have—all of them—as ones that are there to serve you and develop you into a person with ever-increasing impact and value.

This book is not a "think positive" book that will tell you "it is all in your head." Instead, each chapter will walk you through the real experience of my experiment to provide you with building blocks to a more successful life.

Rather than hope things will figure themselves out, this is your opportunity to decide how you are going to deal with the world. This is where you get to decide how you will contribute.

This life is not something to suffer through, tolerate, or merely endure. Our lives give us experiences that are tailor-made for us, which ultimately assist us in reaching our highest potential, experiencing the most good, and becoming a light to those around us.

There has never been a time when this message has been more important than right now. *You* are the answer! In a time when it seems that the loudest voices are violent ones and conflict is disguised in peaceful protest and free speech, it is vital that we take a stand. It is when everything around you seems to lack in integrity that you have to dig deep into your soul and find it in yourself, and change the world right where you are.

Chapter 1
What is Generosity?

Remember there is no such thing as a small act of kindness. Every act creates a ripple with no logical end. —Scott Adams, satirical cartoonist and author

"It's probably not safe to help."

"I don't have time."

"I have better things I need to be doing."

"I am going to be late if I stop."

"They don't really need me."

"I can't make a difference."

"I'm sure someone else will be on their way soon."

"It might look weird if I help."

These thoughts plague our minds as if they were a prosecutor cross-examining us in court, finding clever ways to make us doubt ourselves. These excuses can seem compelling on the surface, but ultimately, they are false. Unfortunately, when we give into our excuses, it keeps us in our "comfort zone" doing what we always do.

After about a week into my experiment, I started to notice a theme in the excuses I gave, which we may even call "reasons" instead of "excuses" in order to lessen the blow of guilt. Reasons have a factual feel to them and give way to the "out of our control" story we tell ourselves. It came down to a matter of time: not so much a lack of time, but a failure to be more intentional with my time. We live in a fast-paced world where everyone has a million things to do, and I am no different.

I seemed to always be running frantically from place to place, whether it was taking my son to soccer practice, taking my daughter to gymnastics, a work meeting, or any number of other things that filled up my day. I was always trying to get things done. If I was not on schedule, I was usually late.

I realized that in order for this experiment to have the outcome I wanted, I needed to be more intentional about my generosity. So I decided to make a list of the specific things I could do to be more intentionally generous.

First, instead of merely being on time (or late), I would plan, when I could, to leave early for my commitments. This would challenge my excuses about not having enough time. Time was a valid excuse until I became intentional about it.

One morning, after making the list, I deliberately set out on my errands early, eager to give myself enough breathing room to vanquish the "not enough time" excuse when it would inevitably raise its ugly head. But could I win against the other excuses in my brain?

I was driving to the store a few miles from my home to buy a screw for my boat trailer to replace the one that had rattled loose and fallen off. I was approaching a stop sign, preparing to turn left onto a fairly busy road. There were no sidewalks on that road, just a thin strip of dirt and gravel alongside a corn field.

A young woman and her little girl, probably about 3 years old, were walking along the dirt strip engulfed in a cloud of dust.

There was a little white pickup truck with them on this narrow strip of dirt swerving at them, making the cloud of dust bigger with each turn of the tire, missing the woman and her child by a few feet. It looked like the person driving the white pickup was just playing around by swerving close to this woman and her kid. Amidst all the traffic, it might have been easy to overlook. But as I watched this scene unfold, as the woman would yank her child's hand to pull her close and out of the way of the truck speeding by them, it became obvious that this woman was distraught. It became apparent—this driver was intentionally trying to hurt this woman and her child.

After the driver passed them the first time, the truck spun around and came back to swerve at her again. And then a third time. The woman and her daughter tried to seek refuge where they could—behind an electrical box—but really, there was nowhere for them to go for protection.

But I could offer help.

I was still sitting at the stop sign waiting for traffic to clear so I could make my turn, with the internal dialogue that had become second nature already churning in my brain. Because I had set my intention to be generous that day, I was acutely aware of the conversation in my head, trying to talk myself out of driving over to help this little family.

Finally the traffic cleared; I had come to the crucial moment of deciding whether to help or to to pass on this opportunity in hopes of finding a different opportunity that would not push me so far out of my comfort zone.

I wish I could say that I immediately made the obvious choice, that I whipped my car around and swooped in to save the woman and her little girl. I wish I could say I acted like a superhero in an action movie.

But even with my new consciousness, I still let my old habits win. When the traffic cleared, I turned left to go about my business, leaving this woman and her troubles in my rearview as I passed her. I was about to leave and never see her again.

In those few seconds, dozens of thoughts ran through my head. "It's not safe." "You will be mocked for offering help." This is the way my brain had been accustomed to working in these situations. Excuses to get out of helping. Excuses I always seemed to listen to before.

But this time, *this time,* I shut that conversation down. Because in this moment, none of that mattered.

A few hundred feet after I passed this opportunity, I turned around, which of course was a lot more inconvenient than just stopping in the first place. But I did it. I turned around. I was about to take that opportunity to be generous. I thought, "What's the worst that could happen?"

In that moment, it was like a light switch had flipped. I realized what I was doing. I wasn't going through the motions. I was making this choice, this commitment to help, letting go of the insecurities I had of looking foolish.

I pulled my vehicle right up to the woman. Before I could even put down my window to speak to her, she flung opened the door, threw her child into the back seat, and then came barreling after. She slammed the door shut and yelled "GO!" We sped away—away from the man in the white pickup truck who had whipped around again to take another run at her.

"Is everything ok?" I asked, knowing full well that it wasn't.

We didn't talk much, but in the little time she spent in my car, I learned that the person driving the white pickup was her ex-boyfriend, who was mentally and emotionally unstable and had tried to hurt her before.

No words needed to be spoken for me to know she appreciated my help that day. The seeds of change were beginning in me.

That experience really drove home the idea that we are down here on earth not as isolated people. We are like different puzzle pieces to the same puzzle. We must connect with each other to be complete.

It seems obvious that the person who benefited from generosity in this story was the woman and her child, but the benefits of generosity go far beyond what's immediately apparent.

Can you imagine the trajectory of the ex-boyfriend's life if he had been successful in hitting her or the little girl? Can you imagine the guilt that would plague his life because of a moment he was not thinking right?

Think about all of the people that loved or depended on that man or woman and how this simple act of generosity may have affected their lives. When I extended generosity to the young woman, I also extended it to all of those who love and care about her. I am sure if we were to take a look into both the woman and her ex-boyfriend's lives, we could start to get a real sense of the impact that one act of generosity could have.

Because I had intentionally set out to be generous that day, I could see the woman and her child as in need, and see myself as in a position to help. And only then could I act.

Stories like these help us realize how powerful our subconscious mind can be, how powerful those habits are that prevent us from creating connections with people.

There was a video taken in China of a two-year-old who had been hit by a car and was lying in the middle of the street. It was bad enough that the person who hit the child didn't stop, but as the video goes on you can see people maneuvering to get around the child rather than stopping to help.

We have all seen videos, or heard stories, about when someone is in trouble and no one stops to help. This is often referred to as the bystander effect. The bystander effect says that individuals are less likely to offer help to a victim when other people are present. The greater the number of bystanders, the less likely it is that any one of them will help. Another factor is diffusion of responsibility; an example of this is when we say "someone else will do it" or "if it was really important someone would have already taken care of it." If we make an honest evaluation of our lives, most of us will find that we have given into the bystander effect. When we are influenced by tendencies like these without giving it any meaningful thought, it can have damaging effects on our ability to be generous.

It seems improbable that there was nobody who had the time to stop and help the child lying in the middle of the street. However, when it's actually time to act, how often do you get outside of your habit zone or the way you have become accustomed to doing things? How often do you let the insecurities of how you will be perceived stop you from asking a stranger if they are okay?

I often wonder what would have happened to the woman and her daughter if I had not stopped on the side of the road for her that day. Many other motorists had not stopped, and I almost didn't.

That day, at the woman's instructions, I pulled my truck into the 7-Eleven parking lot a few miles from where I had picked her up. As we were waiting for the woman's brother to pick her up, I thought of how many opportunities to be generous I had missed. How many times have I passed up the opportunity to learn and change because I was not aware of the dialogue going on inside my own head? In the end, it wasn't just the woman and her child this experiment was helping—it was also helping me.

By definition, generosity means being kind and giving. I had gotten into the habit of seeing it as merely giving somebody something, whether it be time, money, or items. Well, I've come to know that perhaps the greatest gift of generosity is the blessings we invite into our life from having a generous mindset.

What is the Generosity Experiment?

This Generosity Experiment was twenty-one comfort zone-busting days of reshaping the way I approached life in order to become a more generous person. In that time, you get the opportunity to challenge your default settings and become a more conscious participant in your own thought process. Perhaps the most important finding from this experience is that you will understand more fully the benefit that generosity can bring to your life.

When faced with an opportunity to give, some may ask, "Is this the smartest way to give? Wouldn't it be smarter to give to a homeless shelter, instead of a homeless person?" Those are some of the same excuses I have given in the past for myself.

This experiment helped me realize that it wasn't about the *smartest* and *best* gift I could give; this was about me learning how to stop saying "no"simply because it was comfortable.

We move through our lives so quickly that "no" becomes our default answer without us even noticing it. Oftentimes we hide behind what is "smart," and it keeps us from doing the thing that can have the most impact and influence.

How many times do you think you get asked for help in a day, whether directly or indirectly? Is it two, three, four, or even five times a day? How many times do you say yes? Maybe one out of five? If we say no often enough, it will soon become part of who we are; it becomes your reflex, something we do without giving it a second thought.

The Generosity Experiment is designed to create a new habit and a new reflex. It requires practice and diligence and focus. Like any new habit—eating better, exercising more, or waking up earlier—adopting generosity requires repetition and practice.

Think of this experiment as as the training you would do before a marathon. You dial in your running, you follow a schedule, you make sure your nutrition is on point. You are focused. Instead of training for a marathon, though, you are training your habits, mindsets, and perspectives so you can run a more generous life. This will be *your* experiment—you get to set your own rules and goals.

You are probably already a giving person; the fact that you are reading this book says something about your desire to be generous. You try to help others, perhaps by helping a friend through a tough time, taking your neighbor cookies, or opening a door for someone, or it might even be bigger things. How do you feel when you give? Pretty spectacular, I'll bet. There are few feelings that compare to the one we get from assisting someone's life for the better.

I've always viewed myself as a fairly generous person. As far back as I can remember, when adults would ask me what I wanted to be when I grew up, I can remember wanting to make a difference and wanting to be a part of something bigger than myself, something that mattered and had purpose. I also had a knowledge that it would take money to not just create comfort and security but that money would be a great multiplier of my purpose.

I concocted all sorts of ideas to make money while also making a difference. I thought about being a teacher, but knew I needed to make more money if I was going to have the impact I wanted to have in the world, so I decided I would own a private school. Later on, I wanted to find a way to house the homeless, so I decided to become a contractor and hire the homeless to work for me.

Most of the ideas that my ten-year-old mind could think of were not entirely realistic. However, the idea of making a difference throughout my life as I have gone through both trials and successes, has woven itself throughout everything I have done. I bet if you look hard enough you will find that theme in your life too.

As I grew to adulthood, I discovered that another one of my passions is connecting with people: talking, understanding the human condition, learning what people go through and why they go through it. I wanted to weave that into my generosity ideas.

Going to Ghana had been on my bucket list, and the last ten years I had felt an increased pull to go there and contribute while also taking part in their culture. The time had finally come that I was going to take my trip. I made travel arrangements through a company that facilitated volunteers traveling abroad to serve in local communities. I had decided to spend ten days learning and serving, and I was excited for this new adventure.

The one thing that stood out most to me was not the stark difference in the living conditions like the deteriorating roads, the lack of technology, or lack of clean water; it was the people's willingness to be generous with their time and their possessions. Time after time, I was amazed by the kindness they not only showed us but the kindness they showed to each other.

One day, I, along with the host Bernard and some of the other locals, was laying bricks that had been made by hand the days before. We were constructing the interior walls of a home. I had the opportunity to meet a man named Kaka while we were working. He was on his way home from his farm when he saw us working. Instead of walking by, he started to help. The exchange between Bernard and Kaka took me by surprise. When Kaka offered his help, there was no hesitation for Bernard to put him to work. The giving and receiving went hand in hand. He didn't just help for a few hours—he stayed the entire day and took on the hardest jobs.

One particular day we had been tasked with taking down a tree that was too close to the house. This tree, as most of the trees in this small village, was not small. It appeared, by the size of it, to have been growing for hundreds of years. It was four feet across, and it shot no less than forty feet into the air. Kaka took the job of sawing it down….by hand. We had our shovels and pick axes to chip away at the roots, but the lionshare of the energy expended that day was used by Kaka. It surprised me to see him show up again the next day to help.

You might ask, why? I know I did.

After watching him, I asked Bernard half-jokingly if Kaka was trying to work off some debt he owed. Bernard told me that this kind of thing was common, not only for Kaka but as a general rule. If there was a need that could be filled, it was. It didn't take a tragedy or dire circumstance for the villagers to jump in and serve. I realized generosity was *who Kaka was*.

My time in Ghana gave me the eyes to see generosity in a completely different way. It became more about seeing other people as I saw myself, as both having needs and capable of filling the needs of others. We are both human and share in the same humanity. We can learn from one another.

Seeing each other with much in common and having so many desires and goals that align, it makes sense to partner with one another in pursuit of getting the most out of this life. As partners in generosity, we can truly see one another. We may not ever be able to be rid of prejudice but we can continually get better at seeing through the eyes of empathy. I can see others as worthy of my generosity, and I can see myself as worthy of their generosity.

After an amazing ten days in Ghana, I arrived home with a new perspective. I had gained such powerful insight and learning experiences, I would be different now!

Or would I?

It was easy for me to see the beauty in the actions of others in a far-off land, away from my everyday life. The generous actions of people I was getting to know for the first time made the contrast so apparent that it was hard to miss, but had it really *changed me*?

Not long after I came home, I realized that although my experience may have had an impact on my thoughts and even shifted my mindset a little, generosity was not something you could develop simply by being a witness to it. It is something that, in order to be cultivated, must be practiced daily.

You see, in the past I would let my internal dialogue win. Many times it is not a choice between doing something right or wrong when it comes to generosity, but it can still feel that way. Anytime we fight the impulse to take action, we have to create a reason why it is okay not to act. We have to dispel the feeling we have of not being consistent with our internal compass, and that can be uncomfortable. The possibility of being generous wasn't necessarily a right or a wrong choice laid out neatly in front of me—and yet, I had come up with all these reasons why it was okay NOT to act. I was not practicing generosity daily or even regularly. Going to Ghana helped my eyes begin to open. Now that I was home, my new perspective would be put to the test.

Internal Dialogue

I had been back from Ghana for about a week and one day I was out running errands. I had just finished up my last stop, and I was coming home about three o'clock in the afternoon. I was just getting off the freeway onto the road that would take me home. This was an ordinary day, and the drive was just like the many I had taken before.

On this particular exit, there always seems to be someone—though not always the same person—holding a sign asking for money. My daughter calls them "sign holders." At many of the exits where I live, there are sign holders, and their signs usually explain their struggles.

I had driven by these people many times, probably hundreds of times, before. Each time I passed them by, I had an interesting internal dialogue. I told myself something like, "It's okay if you don't give to them, because you give in other ways," or "It's okay if you don't give because you don't know what they might spend that money on." This thought process was an attempt to help myself feel okay about not giving, to justify my inaction despite the feeling that I should do something. Most of us go through this justification process on some level, and likely do it so often that we don't even notice it anymore.

But, on this particular day I started to evaluate the level of my generosity. Had Africa changed me? Was I living up to the example of Kaka? Was giving part of who I was?

Apparently not, or at least I realized that the image I had of myself and the reality of who I really was, were a little further apart then I wanted them to be. I had been full of excuses and not much action.

How often do we make excuses to not be generous? I actually said "no" quite a bit. It wasn't just a one-time thing with homeless people or the sign holders on the street. It happened in other ways, too. How many times had I debated tipping the customary amount, or tipping extra? Even if it was just five dollars, it was still a battle in my head. "What is expected of me?" My head always seemed to be flooded with reasons of why it was okay not to do something. Once I recognized this thought process for what it was, I noticed it popping up more and more throughout my life. "Slow down, stop! Why can't I just be generous?" I asked myself.

I thought I was a generous person, but I was passing by dozens opportunities to give generously. And by refusing to give, I was also passing up the opportunity receive the blessings of being generous and the joy of forming human connections.

This is not to say that there can't be productive dialogue inside our heads that might determine that a certain act won't provide generosity. The point is, we should be conscious of the dialogue, evaluate it, and then make an informed choice.

When we over think the part we should play in generosity, we think around the opportunity to be generous, so that we can feel good about not helping. This feeling can mislead us. Instead of simply acting generously, we tell ourselves all the reasons we are already good enough so that we don't feel guilty about not acting.

That isn't to say that you should act on *every* opportunity to be generous. There are times when it is best to act and there are times when it is best not to. I started my experiment to discover how to tell the difference between these two types of opportunities, and how to take action as often as possible.

Now that a whole new world has opened up for me, I want to share it with you.

Chapter 1 Challenges:

- *This week, keep your ears open for the excuses you hear from other people that keep them from living generously. Write them down and avoid using them yourself.*

- *Next time you find yourself making excuses, take note. What does your inner dialogue say? What are some of the things that you should listen for that prevent you from living out the Generosity Experiment?*

- *Name three things that you can do TODAY to be more generous. Who needs your help? Where are the places that you should look?*

Chapter 2
Gratitude First

*Gratitude is not only the greatest of all
virtues, but the parent of all the others.
—Marcus Tullius Cicero, Roman orator
106 B.C. to 43 B.C.*

Gratitude and generosity are extremely intertwined. If you take any virtue in its purest form, you'll see gratitude wrapped up inside it.

But, most of us are missing the point of gratitude entirely.

You might have heard of gratitude journals, gratitude lists, and gratitude meditations. These are all structured attempts to find joy and happiness through gratitude. They usually start off by asking you to identify what you are grateful for. While each of these things is beneficial and can help us to grow our gratitude, they are also only focused on one aspect of gratitude. We will talk about which parts are missing later in this chapter.

Because of this, they handicap our ability to fully implement gratitude in our lives. The resultant "gratitude industry," then, only gets at the surface level of gratitude. I would even go so far as to say that it is counterfeit.

Rarely does anyone in the self-help or the gratitude industry talk about *what* we should be grateful for.

What should we be grateful for? It's an elementary question. Perhaps you're thinking *"nobody should be telling me what I should be grateful for"*, that it should be a personal decision. However, every guiding principle—from generosity to gratitude to humility—has "rules" that need to be followed in order to reach its full intended benefit.

For example, to be full of integrity, you must be honest and treat others the way you want to be treated. That's the cardinal rule for integrity. Forgiveness, we are told, is to be given to everyone. In order for you to be free of the restraints of bitterness and resentment, you cannot pick and choose whom to forgive. It is required that we forgive everyone always, and the quicker we can do that, the happier we will be. Just like integrity and forgiveness, gratitude has its rules, too.

Let's dissect gratitude so we can take a closer look at it and figure out its rules. In the process, we will also be learning more about generosity.

The Comparison Trap

There is a fairly common prescription for gratitude: the idea of "aiming up" and "comparing down."

"Comparing down" is the act of comparing your own situation to the situations of those who are less fortunate than you. In contrast, "comparing up" is comparing your situation to the situations of people who are more fortunate than you. Many of us can see the problem with comparing up because of the effect it has on us. Rather than enjoying our circumstances, we begin to notice all of the things that we don't have. It creates envy and we end up wanting what other people have. It crushes our spirit.

When we feel bad about ourselves, we tend to look for evidence to support our feelings of inadequacies and shortcomings. Rather than working on ourselves and elevating ourselves honestly, we just compare ourselves to someone who is smarter, wealthier, or stronger. We lose perspective of where we stand. Instead of appreciating where we are and we obsess about where we're not. Comparing up is not only futile, but self-destructive.

In this method, comparing down isn't an excuse to stop pushing ahead and striving. That's where "aiming up" comes in. Most of us know we cannot get where we want to be in life by aiming (or dreaming) small. Aiming at a target in front of you will propel you to play your best possible game.

Anytime we allow comparison to play into our gratitude and happiness we are playing a dangerous game.

Confucius said that "the hardest thing of all is to find a black cat in a dark room, especially if there is no cat." When we compare up or down to find any level of gratitude, gratitude will feel elusive and hard to find, just like the cat. The only indication of where we are is when we smack into a wall. Gratitude, when it is understood, is like flipping on the light and seeing everything for what it actually is, instead of seeing ourselves only in comparison to others.

Since comparing up is so unpleasant, we look for another way. We are constantly surrounded by others, and, through technology, we have access to even more stories of people around the world. As a result, we have a tendency to take the short and often short lived, route to gratitude. We flip the comparison—instead of comparing up, we compare down. We look for people "lesser than" us in order to feel grateful.

I can remember sitting at the dinner table as a child, with all the food I didn't like still left on my plate. At some point, either my mom or my dad would guilt me into gratitude for the food in front of me by bringing to my attention the starving kids around the world. My parents were probably no different than yours.

How many times have you said this to yourself: "At least I'm not ____." Fill in the blank with whatever you like: Terminally ill. Homeless. Jobless. Anyone who is deemed "without" something. In essence, we appear to be grateful by thinking, "I have it bad, but think of the people who have it worse than I do."

The big question is this: Does comparing down really lead to gratitude? Not a chance. Comparing down is an empty tool that gives us a false sense of gratitude.

I have come to realize that true principles and virtues hold up no matter the situation.

Returning home from Ghana, I had many conversations with people curious about my experience. After hearing about the living conditions of some of the people I encountered there, the most common comment was, "I bet seeing that makes you more grateful for what you have." The answer I thought in my head was completely opposite of what the socially accepted response was. As I heard this comment time and time again, I reflected on the people I had met in Jasikan. If they were not less grateful for what they had because I had more, then why is it that so many of us think we should be more grateful when we see someone with less?

Whether you think you Have more or less than someone is dependant on your perspective. From my view, a big reason there were so many happy and grateful people in this small village was that a large majority of them did not have access to the advances in technology like internet, social media, and television, which provide a 24/7 opportunity to compare.

Often in life it is not because we are lazy that we take the most convenient choice, but rather it is because we are not aware that there is a far better choice that lies beneath the convenient choice. This is the case with our knee-jerk reactions to compare.

The tendency to compare up or down has been ingrained in us. Because so many people do it, we model it on a daily basis, becoming quick and efficient at comparing ourselves to others. And, to help ourselves feel better about comparing, we mask it as gratitude.

Comparison can backfire on us when our lives don't go as planned. Bankruptcy is not a fun experience and can be a particularly low time for people. It was no different for me. In 2010, I had just come off of a failed business that tanked along with many other investment and real estate businesses. We held on for as long as we could until it was clear that we were not going to be able to recover financially. Because much of the business was tied up with our personal finances, we were going to have to file personal bankruptcy.

I felt that there was not anyone for me to compare down to. At the time, I felt like my situation was the worst thing that could happen to someone. The thought of letting down my family became a horrific reality to me.

I remember the first Christmas after our bankruptcy had been finalized. We were barely scraping enough cash together to pay for groceries and keep the lights on, we had surrendered our car, and we were in the process of having our house foreclosed on. My wife and I had two kids at the time, ages four and three. They were old enough to have certain expectations about Christmas, such as having presents waiting for them under the tree on Christmas morning.

In a desperate attempt to give our children something to open, we gathered everything we had around the house that could be returned to the store. Batteries, light bulbs, and anything else we could find that hadn't yet been opened. We returned anything that we could get the store to give us money for.

On Christmas morning, our kids tore off the wrapping paper to find fruit snacks and Band-Aids with their favorite characters. This was a low point for me, feeling like I had failed at business, had let my wife down, and couldn't even provide a true Christmas for my kids. At the time I could not imagine anyone being in a worse situation than I was. It doesn't matter if I was choosing not to see or if I was blinded by my self-pity, at the time I could not find anyone to compare down to. Because comparison was the familiar path I knew to gratitude, it seemed impossible to have gratitude for anything in my life at that point.

Many of us will go through times when we feel we have it so bad that we can't think of anyone who has it worse. In times like these, with no option to compare down, how can we still find gratitude? If you are homeless, and can't find anyone else worse off than you, are you not allowed to be grateful?

Looking back, I can see that I had plenty to be grateful for that Christmas. Even the situation that brought up feelings of insurmountable self-pity, I could have been grateful for. Today I see that situation as my turning point. It became the launching pad to living more abundantly and introspectively. It changed me for the better and without it I would not have been given the feedback from my life that I needed to become a better person. Today, I am more empathetic to the situations of other people. I value giving others the benefit of the doubt, and possibly the most powerful truth that came from that time is that I could believe in myself no matter what.

Using the comparison method for gratitude failed me in this circumstance, because it is not built on a firm foundation. Comparing down was based on how I felt and on my ability to step outside of myself. At the time, I was too consumed by self-pity to step outside myself. I was blinded to the massive learning opportunity right in front of me.

If my daughter came to me and told me she didn't feel pretty, would it be appropriate to say, "Oh, sweetie! Go find someone uglier than you to feel better!" No way! But we do this type of comparison all the time in other situations. There is no difference whether we are comparing down about money, health, or even beauty; we are so conditioned to compare that we don't even think about it. Instead, we tend to paint our comparisons with pretty words to make us feel better about it. We justify it and continue on with our lives.

Even if we aren't comparing out loud, many of us are doing it in our thoughts. Do you ever show up at a small gathering and compare your own clothing choices to everyone else's? Perhaps you compare your body to someone else's less fit body? Or maybe you compare your intelligence to another person's? That is not a healthy way to feel gratitude.

Comparison has been around for as long as history has been recorded. The Bible tells stories about how Adam and Eve offered sacrifices to God, a practice that was then taught to their children Cain and Abel. Cain grew vegetables and grain while Abel raised sheep. Like many siblings, the two boys didn't always get along.

When Cain saw that his sacrifice of vegetables and grain couldn't compare to his brother Abel's sacrifice of sheep, he fell into the comparison trap. When God decided that what Abel had put on the table was a more desireable sacrifice than what Cain had put on the table to sacrifice, Cain saw Abel as a threat. Instead of going to his brother with a mind open to learn, Cain decided to kill him so that he wouldn't have to feel the discomfort that comes when we compare up.

We all want to know where we stand. In Abraham Maslow's hierarchy of human needs,[1] there are five different levels of needs. Right after the first two—physical needs such as food and then safety needs such as shelter—are love and acceptance. Everyone is looking for love and acceptance in some form or another. In our attempt to feel accepted, we often resort to comparison, just like Cain did.

Our minds start to wander. Why does this person have more than I do? Is it because he is more loved? Then we start to judge our own love and belonging based on possessions and other visible factors. It's like we're creating our own pecking order. Our accomplishments don't mean as much. We start regretting even the good things in our lives.

After we have calculated our so-called worth, we then determine how grateful we should be, and who we are better than, or who is better than us, and who is more loved.

Most often the judgments that we feel from other people, which we might call self-righteousness, are not judgments based on our own actions or lifestyle. They are instead rooted in someone else's misguided attempt to feel love and belonging. You might be a tool for someone to define their belonging, or a tool for someone to feel that they are loved. Either way, it is an attempt for them to determine how they are doing and how deserving they are of love.

Here's the thing that keeps us trapped in this mindset: We don't even realize that we do it. It operates on a subconscious level, because of our fundamental and innate desire to feel love, belonging, and acceptance.

This happens so easily because our brains are good at learning and storing information for use without active thought.

When I was first learning how to drive, I would actively think about every step needed to just back out of the driveway. It was such an intense maneuver for a new driver that my driver's education teacher had a checklist of things that should be done before and during the process.

- Turn off the music
- Adjust your rearview mirrors
- Look over both shoulders

- Remove foot off brake and ease back
- Steer through the

As a new driver, that list relieved a great deal of my tension. When we are first learning to drive, everything is new and our senses are on high alert. Today, the things listed on that checklist are stored in the back of my mind and are second nature to me because I drive regularly.

Comparing is no different, but it starts early in our lives and happens a lot more frequently than backing out a car. Invitations to compare bombard us on a daily basis, whether it is an advertisement trying to get us to feel bad about not having what the guy on the television has, or a charity trying to get us to feel compelled to give by helping us to compare down. It might be at work, at home among members of your family.

We think we are being benevolent and virtuous by comparing down to determine our gratitude. In reality, we are putting ourselves further into this trap of not appreciating or accepting true gratitude. Counterfeit gratitude is like the storm-tossed waves that ebb in and out. As a true principle, gratitude never wavers. You can be grateful always, 100 percent of the time.

Thank You For The Fleas

In her book *The Hiding Place*, Corrie Ten Boom and her sister Betsie had been imprisoned by the Nazis for hiding Jews behind the wall of their Holland home. The conditions in the Nazi prison were nearly unbearable.

Corrie writes:

> *Barracks 8 was in the quarantine compound. Next to us—perhaps as a deliberate warning to newcomers—were located the punishment barracks. From there, all day long and often into the night, came the sounds of hell itself. They were not the sounds of anger, or of any human emotion, but of a cruelty altogether detached: blows landing in regular rhythm, screams keeping pace. We would stand in our ten-deep ranks with our hands trembling at our sides, longing to jam them against our ears, to make the sounds stop.*
>
> *It grew harder and harder. Even within these four walls there was too much misery, too much seemingly pointless suffering. Every day something else failed to make sense, something else grew too heavy.*
>
> *When they were moved to Barracks 28, the punishment barracks, Corrie was horrified by the fact that their reeking, straw-bed platforms swarmed with fleas. How could they live in such a place?*

It was Betsie who found a purpose for the fleas:

> " *'Rejoice always, pray constantly, give thanks in all circumstances; for this is the will of God*

in Christ Jesus.' That's it, Corrie! That's His answer. 'Give thanks in all circumstances!' That's what we can do. We can start right now to thank God for every single thing about this new barracks!'"

I stared at her; then around me at the dark, foul-aired room...

The two sisters thanked God that they were together. They thanked God they had a Bible. They even thanked God for the horrible crowds of prisoners, that more people would be able to hear God's Word. And then, Betsie thanked God for the fleas.

The fleas! This was too much. "Betsie, there's no way even God can make me grateful for a flea."

"'Give thanks in all circumstances,'" she quoted. "It doesn't say, in pleasant circumstances. Fleas are part of this place where God has put us."

And so we stood between tiers of bunks and gave thanks for fleas. But this time I was sure Betsie was wrong.2

It turned out that Betsie was not wrong; the fleas were a nuisance, but a blessing after all. The women were able to have Bible studies in the barracks with a great deal of freedom, never bothered by supervisors coming in and harassing them. They finally discovered that it was the fleas that kept those supervisors out.

Gratitude and Value Systems

A few years ago, when my daughter was seven years old, she loved Disneyland (and still does). On her seventh birthday, we decided to surprise her with a trip to Disneyland. There was something special to her about Minnie Mouse. We made sure to get pictures with all the other characters, and we even had breakfast in Goofy's kitchen. But at the end of our trip all she wanted was a stuffed Minnie Mouse toy. To cap off her birthday weekend, we got her the doll. She played with it constantly, and it made her happy.

Of course, our three-year-old daughter watched her. We could see the wheels in her head turning as she watched her sister play with that Minnie doll. She must have been thinking, "If I have that, I'll be just as happy!" There was a lot of fighting and many tears shed over that doll.

As their parents, without realizing what we were doing, we fell into the comparison trap; we helped our children compare up or down as it catered to our needs in order to keep the peace.

In an effort to get her to share we said things like, "You should be grateful you have this doll because your sister doesn't," and "There are plenty of kids who don't have toys," and "You should feel bad for her and share it with her."

At that point, our three-year-old felt entitled to play with the doll simply because of pity. At the same time, our seven-year-old felt privileged. Thinking about it in that perspective causes me to cringe. We love them both the same!

So what was the outcome? We broke down and bought our three-year-old the same doll so the two could be "equal," but then something interesting happened. After about a week or so, our three-year-old lost interest in the Minnie doll and it found its way to the bottom of the toy chest and she rarely played with it thereafter.

Because of the way our seven-year-old processed Disneyland, the doll meant so much to her. There was a lot of emotion attached to Minnie. However, that emotion was not something our three-year-old possessed toward Disneyland or the doll. There was no possible way for her to have the same experience with the Minnie doll that her older sister had.

It was impossible that if our three-year-old had what her sister had, she would be equally happy. That reality didn't exist! It was an illusion. Our happiness and gratefulness is all relative to our own mindset and personality, not to someone else's perspective or thought process.

This scenario is telling of the human condition. Just as it happens with children, it happens with adults, only with different objects of jealousy—money, relationships, body types, looks, jobs, you name it.

Have you ever thought, "I'll be happy when …" I will be happy when I have a new car, or lose ten more pounds, or pay off my mortgages. We think we'll be grateful when that particular thing finally comes true. When we go through this thought process, we put conditions on our gratitude and conditions on our happiness.

There is danger in that kind of thinking. In order to get through your day, you have to identify the people who have more or less than you in order to be grateful, which breeds mood swings and entitlement. "I am not going to be generous to him—he should be generous to me." It is impossible to compare down without also comparing up.

I was in Nashville at a business conference and took advantage of one of the breaks to run out to one of the food trucks to buy an ice cream cone. While waiting in line, there was a lady in front of me who paid with a twenty dollar bill and, to my surprise, paid for me as well!

At the time, I wondered what prompted her to do that. I didn't appear as someone who needed help or charity. I was most likely at same convention she was, I was dressed nicely, and I was in line buying an ice cream cone. Obviously I had the money to pay for something frivolous. Why did she feel the need to pay for me?

She didn't see that comparison model. The woman didn't look at my outward appearance and use that as evidence as to whether I was "deserving" of her help or not. She saw me as a person, and as worthy of her generosity.

Alexander Pope said, "Whenever I find a great deal of gratitude in a poor man, I take it for granted there would be as much generosity if he were a rich man."

How many opportunities do we miss out on to be generous because we are too busy comparing ourselves up or down? How many opportunities do we miss out on because we are deciding if another person is worthy or unworthy of our generosity?

The *way* we are generous to a wealthy person may be different from the way we are generous to someone who is struggling financially, but we might miss the conversation or kind word that a wealthy person is in need of if we are caught up in the comparison trap. Likewise, if you have money and you see a person who is struggling with finances as someone to compare down to, it is hard not to become fixated on that and miss the opportunities to be generous in a much more impactful way.

Don't compare just because it is easy.

Anyone who seeks out shortcomings in someone else will find them. If I look hard enough, I can always find someone to compare myself to. Just because you do more, or struggle more, doesn't make you more or less deserving. *Everyone is deserving.*

So, have you decided to be done comparing? How do you stop a subconscious thought process?

3 Steps to Lasting Gratitude

"What if today we were just grateful for everything?" —Charlie Brown

A few years ago I was attending a business seminar designed to help entrepreneurs navigate the inevitable obstacles and ups and downs that come with any business. The facilitator of one particular session addressed a large group of us with a question: "If I asked what you should be grateful for, what would you tell me?" As thoughts of some of the failures our collective group had experienced in both our personal and professional life were carefully considered, one of the men in the group raised his hand. He gave an answer that I could tell he felt was true but couldn't quite wrap his head around.

He said, "Everything."

It is true, we should be grateful for everything, but how good are we at actually putting that into action? When we name our blessings, are we just grabbing the low-hanging fruit and listing the stuff that is easy to be grateful for? When we think of what we're grateful for, we often first think of our health, our home, our country, our family, etc. Of course we should be grateful for those things. But we shouldn't stop there. Are we intentionally leaving things off of our gratitude list? Or are we not even aware of how much we truly have to be grateful for?

There are three key steps to being able to fill our lives with gratitude and happiness. The saying "a grateful heart is a happy heart" applies here. The level of gratitude we experience directly corresponds to the level of purpose and happiness we can find in all of life's circumstances.

1. Accept everything in your present reality as a gift

Think about everything going on in your life right now. Are you grateful for *all* of it?

When you are grateful for something—even if it doesn't seem like a positive thing—then you can learn from it. On the other hand, if you resent your circumstances, you close yourself off from a potential learning moment. For example, if you are in a class and you don't like or respect the teacher, then you just want the class to be over. You won't learn anything, because you'll be spending the entire class period watching the clock, tick-tock! This is the difference between getting through your experiences and letting your experiences pass through you.

Allowing our experiences to pass through us means that we not only learn to love the opportunity, but we also develop a love for the people who played a part in making the opportunity possible. It's easy to love ourselves and others when life is easy and carefree, but the true test comes when we are going through something hard. These are the times we want to make the exception, playing games to rationalize why this one experience is going to stay in the resentment column. As long as we hold people or circumstances in contempt, we make it almost impossible to learn the lessons they have to teach us that are right in front of us.

Think of it as classifying your life experiences into one of three of the following categories:

- **Positive Experiences/The Vehicles**

    Picture a jar of candy that has the best stuff on the top, so that you grab the most flavorful and sugary kinds of candy first. We will call this type of candy the first ⅓, or the positive experiences. We use these experiences as our "vehicles" to our happy place. These are the experiences that we typically use to feel good about our lives, our relationships, and ourselves. We can easily identify these as good and worthy of being grateful for. This is what I refer to as the "low-hanging fruit." Yes, we should be grateful for these opportunities, but they also require the least amount of growth. Examples could be a bonus at work, all A's on a report card, or a beautiful, sunny day.

- **Insignificant Experiences/The Irrelevant**

    The second ⅓ of experience in the candy jar of life is the insignificant or irrelevant opportunities. At face value, these don't make us feel better or worse. Our days are made up of hundreds of these moments. Since there are so many of these types of experiences, it's easy to go on autopilot through them. If we are not aware that these experiences exist to make us better and provide opportunities to grow, our gratitude for them will never materialize. These are the experiences that most often get ignored and unacknowledged, and typically we are unintentional in our thoughts or attitudes in these moments. These are the most abundant of all the experiences and often contain vital hidden lessons for growth and additional awareness. Examples could be the beating of our hearts, the considerate actions offered to us by the countless people we interact with each day, the person who showed up for their job as a barista so we could get our morning coffee, and other things we don't even think about because we see or take part in them all the time.

- **Negative Experiences/The Obstacles**

The last ⅓ is at the bottom of the candy jar, and it requires more effort to be grateful for. These are the negative opportunities or what we perceive as being the obstacles to our gratitude and happiness. These experiences often provide the most profound results, because they give us opportunities for self-reflection and growth that cannot be accessed except through hardship or pain. This bottom third takes the most work. As we become aware of these experiences, it can feel scary, but there are blessings awaiting you at the end. If you choose to ignore these opportunities, then they will act as weights holding you down.

This is not advice to think positive and look on the bright side but rather taking the proverbial elephant in the room by the tail (your hard thing), learning why it is there and then harnessing its power to propel into a more passionate, more connected life. This takes you from playing the victim role to taking the lead in your life.

Most of the time we are so busy dancing around the elephant in the room looking for other things to put on our gratitude list meanwhile the elephant is sitting right in front of the doorway that leads us to happiness. Without acknowledging it and having gratitude for it we won't be able to get past it.

These "negative" things are what we usually leave off our gratitude list and wish were different. We would never make a list of things we are ungrateful for, because we have an innate knowledge that gratitude should be attached to everything. So, instead, we just leave these obstacles off our gratitude list. But, these moments of ingratitude tend to find a way to creep back into our lives as bad habits and limiting beliefs.

Gratitude can give our pain a purpose. Accepting everything in your life as a gift can prove to be a difficult task at times, especially when we experience particularly painful and trying times. When you are intentionally grateful for something, you give permission for the lesson to appear. When something feels unpleasant, we tend to bury those experiences. In the end, it is hard to find value or purpose in this type of negative experience, the kind located at the bottom of the jar. Gratitude bridges the gap between the negative experiences that hold us back and the necessary lessons that you need to learn in order to grow from those experiences.

2. Accept that you are the only one with the authority to improve what you have to be grateful for

If all we do with our gratitude is put it on a list and look at it when times get tough, then we diminish the effect it can have in our life.

Once you have accepted everything in our life as a gift, the next step is to learn from it. Learning the lessons that will benefit our lives requires that we take 100 percent accountability for the circumstances we find ourselves in.

Blame vs. Accountability

How we respond to our circumstances will be the biggest indicator of whether our lives will improve or not. Generally we have two routes we can choose from when it comes to our individual circumstances. These are blame and accountability. Although these two terms seem to be similar, they produce remarkably different outcomes.

Blame is assigning something to the past to justify our present circumstances. Accountability is evaluating our choices to create a better future. This doesn't mean that blame isn't a useful tool. But most often when blame is used first, before we have taken accountability and evaluated our choices, it makes it very difficult to face the change we must make ourselves if our life is to improve.

There are two types of people that emerge when we take a look at our lives and start to identify all that we have to be grateful for: the blameologist and the accountant.

- *The Blameologist*

    This person concedes gratitude for only the most obvious low-hanging fruit. Instead of also finding gratitude in the more difficult situations, they instead seek to place the blame for those situations on others. Blame can be placed on a person or a set of circumstances—either way, the blameologist looks to other people for solutions and blames them if the solution is not found. In order to be grateful, the blameologist has to find someone or something to change their negative situation.

    There is one simple truth for every difficulty, and that is *you* are the only common denominator to all of your problems. You cannot find a lasting solution until you look inward first. The solution might still require the help of other people, but if it does not start with you questioning your own actions and mindset, chances are there will be plenty of people to blame, but you will still be getting the same negative results.

Take a second to evaluate what it takes for you to be happy. Got it? Okay. Look down your list to see if other people's actions are one of your prerequisites for happiness. If other people's actions are a requirement to make you happy, what are the chances you will be happy?

- *The Accountant*

  The first place an accountant looks for answers is themselves. They realize that it is much easier to change their own actions to get what they want than to try to change someone else's. An accountant can identify and accept blame if it is warranted, because the accountant's primary goal is not to place blame or to make sure the other party knows what they did was wrong. Instead, the accountant's goal is to take responsibility for their choices and ultimately they take responsibility for their happiness. They look for what could be done differently in the future to increase their level of happiness.

Most people fit into one of these categories, or both. Take a moment and reflect; which one are you? When have you displayed behavior that fits into one of these clear categories?

Our society gets blaming and accounting confused all the time. Usually the more difficult or tragic the circumstance, the harder it is to separate the two behaviors because we add emotion into the equation. But no matter how dramatic the circumstance, an accountant will always have far better potential to improve his or her life and prevent unwanted situations from happening again.

As we begin to take on the role of being a self-directed accountant for our lives, we get a glimpse of how grateful we really can be.

3. You have the responsibility to increase your gratitude

Gratitude is an action word. It only comes alive when you practice it. We tend to take care of those things for which we are truly grateful.

It is not enough for us just to survive in this life. It is, to each of us, a responsibility to do something worthwhile in society. Each of us has light we gain by learning from our experiences. This light, while illuminating our own path, can also be the light for another's path as well. It is our responsibility to continually acquire more of it, because the more light we each have as individuals, the more light we will be able to shine into this darkened world. To increase our light, we must educate and grow ourselves.

There is an interesting story in the Bible, the story of the man with many talents. Talents were a unit of measurement and one talent is estimated to be equivalent to the income of a lifetime for a person at that time.

The ancient story tells that there was a master with three servants. He got them together one day and said to the three, "I've got these talents and I want you to take them and see what you can do with them while I am gone. When I get back we'll get together go over the progress to see how you did." He gave five talents to one servant, two talents to another, and one talent to the third.

When the master came back, he got the three servants together and asked them how it went with the talents.

The master asked of the first servant, "Your five talents, what happened with them?"

That servant said, "I took the five talents that you gave me and I put them to work. It was a hard at first, but that's when I got going and I worked hard. Things really got rolling and the five talents turned into eight then nine, ten. In the end, I doubled my talents from five to ten."

The master, with a pleased look, said to his servant, "Well done."

To the next servant he said, "I gave you two talents, what happened?"

That servant said, "It was about the same for me, I put those two talents to work and it was hard at first. But that's when I put in the work and the talents grew to three and then to four." He said, "I doubled my talents from two to four."

The master, with the same look as he gave the first, said, "Well done."

To the last servant the master said, "I gave you one talent, what happened?"

That servant said, "Well, I took that talent you gave me and I carefully wrapped it and I dug a hole and I buried it, because I was afraid that it might get lost or stolen. I was also worried that others might think it not fair that I received a talent when they did not, and this is why I hid it in the ground. Fortunately, nobody got it. I knew you were going to be here today so I dug it up and brought it here." As he presented the talent to the master, he said, "Here it is safely wrapped. I did not lose it while you were gone."

According to the story the master said, "Take that one talent away from him and give it to the man who has ten."

This story might pull at your moral logic. You might say, "Well that's not fair, that guy only had one talent. It is not right that the man with ten would get more while the man with one would have his taken away. It ought to be more even."

We don't have to like this lesson, but it would be in our best interest to learn it. It is to say that whatever you do not employ, you forfeit. Whatever you don't use, you lose. A limb immobilized for a long while is atrophied, losing not only muscle but function. The same thing that goes for your limbs goes for your mind, and it goes for all the human virtues. Ambition unused, declines. passions unused, diminish. Faith unused, decrease. Energy unused, dissipates.

This is a law that gets proven time and again in our lives. As soon as we get complacent with our gratitude, when we have accepted that we are grateful enough as is, it is no different then the servant who buried his talent. Not only will we not be able to enjoy the blessing of increased gratitude, but we will have entitlement and resentment creep in to take the place of gratitude in our hearts.

How many times have we been in the shoes of the third servant? We make up excuses as to why it is okay to stay where we are with our life, not increasing our income, not increasing our available time, not increasing our knowledge or skills. We place blame on God, the government, our parents, and politics. We use them as excuses not to improve our lives.

Sometimes just being more intentional about what we see and how we choose to see it can increase our gratefulness. When it rains, it rains on everybody, but each person has a different perspective of the rain. Instead of wishing your circumstances away, ask yourself this question: "What does this make possible?" This mindset can unlock the learning experience that may be necessary for the growth you desire.

When I was in Ghana, we had the opportunity to take many walks through the villages. There were dirt paths that meandered in between and around the handmade adobe homes. Most of the homes had bamboo fences that separated their land from the land that surrounded them. It was astounding that the people were so grateful for their living environment.

It made such a deep impression on me because these same living conditions would cause so many in first world countries to complain,and to sit comfortably in the victim role.

Gratitude is what inspires us to improve what we have. It is not only void of complaint and resentment, but it cultivates the desire to hold precious every moment, possession, and relationship. As I took these little strolls through the villages, I noticed that the homeowners were sweeping the dirt pathways that surrounded their homes and led up to their doorways. Many of these homeowners fashioned brooms made of straw and bamboo sticks. Meticulously, they would clean their dirt paths, brushing aside the leaves and sticks.

Beauty is subjective. Perhaps the beauty that inspires us to do more, to be more, to love more, and to give more is the type of beauty that is born out of gratitude. Why did seeing these dirt paths so carefully cared for inspire me? It was because it was in such contrast to what I had been conditioned to think. Subconsciously, I had allowed myself to believe that someone who lived this way had less to be grateful for.

This was a freeing moment for me. It did not teach me to be more grateful for my cement sidewalks because others have only dirt paths. Instead it taught me that I could be grateful no matter what. It taught me that being grateful for what I have and improving it, amplifying it, and increasing it is the key to happiness. The focus is not just to have more, it is to have more to be grateful for. As we increase what we have to be grateful for, it empowers us to have more to share and to play a part in increasing what others have to be grateful for as well.

When we take steps to increase or to make better that which we have in our lives, we take gratitude from an inanimate emotion to an animated way of life.

Chapter 2 Challenges:

- *Determine the gifts have you been given in your life that have crafted you into the person you are today. Write them down!*

- *What are the the circumstances in your bottom ⅓ (the Negative Experiences) that you haven't dealt with yet? Reflect on how you can turn those experiences into an opportunity for growth.*

- *Begin with the practical. Take two practical actions today to show your gratitude to someone in your life. What bitterness in your life could be shifted into gratitude?*

Chapter 3
A Generous Disposition

But I give best when I give from that deeper place; when I give simply, freely, and generously, and sometimes for no particular reason. I give best when I give from my heart.
— *Steve Goodier, author of* Lessons of the Turtle

As you become more aware of situations to be generous in and people to be generous to that you might have previously overlooked, you'll be able to see what you've been missing. Your new perspective may also be overwhelming at first. You'll soon see opportunities everywhere you turn—in your home and at the grocery store, while you're driving or even just browsing online. It will seem as though the opportunities had been hiding all this time, and now they are revealed.

I decided to dedicate twenty-one days of taking every opportunity I was presented with to be generous. I wanted to be a more generous person, and this twenty-one-day experiment was going to be a time for me to retrain my heart and mind to create new habits. These twenty-one days were the training I needed to develop the skills to live a more generous life.

Keith Mano, a *National Review* columnist, shared a story that might be similar to what you will feel as you become more aware of the generosity opportunities that are all around you:

> Getting rid of blindness, I'm told, is not such a bargain after all. Human eyes, you see—even when healed physically—still need training and rigorous practice before they can transmit what is "real" and "not real" back to the brain. It doesn't much matter how long you've been sightless either: a decade or so of blindness and your cerebral cortex has to be completely reprogrammed, as if from infanthood. On opening his eyes, the healed seer confronts a nonsensical, frightful, and, well, Cubist landscape. Over that shattered universe he must stubbornly impose the familiar 3D grid we live in.
>
> Virgil, age fifty and blind since childhood, has had "successful" eye surgery. Five weeks later he "often felt more disabled than he had felt when he was blind...Steps posed a special hazard, because all he could see was a confusion, a flat surface of parallel and crisscrossing lines; he could not see them (although he knew them) as solid objects going up or coming down in three dimensional space."

Furthermore, Virgil "would pick up details incessantly—an angle, an edge, a colour, a movement—but he would not be able to synthesize them, to form a complex perception at a glance. This was one reason the cat, visually, was so puzzling: he would see the paw, a nose, the tail, an ear, but could not see all of them together, the cat as a whole." And, as his wife noted, "Virgil finally put a tree together—he now knows that the trunk and leaves go together to form a complete unit."[3]

There were times in my Generosity Experiment when I felt like Virgil. I had all the tools, but getting them to work together properly was not as simple as it seemed, at least at first. Generosity is a complex and personal experience, and each of our journeys will be accordingly unique. In the days following the Experiment, I continued to learn and to synthesize my individual experiences into one cohesive lesson. Each day, I continue to "see better" and to live in a more generous way.

At times, it may feel like you're downstream from a broken dam, like you're drowning already but the water continues to keep pouring over you—you simply can't keep up. It's a normal feeling to have. But you need to stick with it, because it gets easier! In the beginning you will be working muscles that have not been worked in a long time, and you might feel sore, and even a little fatigued. This, too, is okay, because you're not just trying to act generous, you're trying to *become* a generous person.

This experiment is not supposed to reflect everyday life, but serves instead as the preparation for a test. That test is life itself. This experiment is your time to see what works and what doesn't work in your own life. It is a time to create new habits and develop the skills to know the answers to the questions on the test. Getting the right answers will make for a much happier and more fulfilled life.

After the experiment, you'll be better equipped to decide how you will be generous thereafter, and you will have created a larger receptacle to receive all of the benefits of generosity.

The blessing of generosity comes not so much from each action, but from where our heart is. Once we become more aware of how and when generously makes itself available to us, it becomes more important to act on the opportunities when we feel prompted to serve. There are times when one thing will pull harder on me than another, and it is these times I am grateful for having strengthened my reflex and resolve to act.

The sense that we have to serve will not be the only thing that will color our landscape. Each person will have many other responsibilities in his or her life to attend to. When we choose not to act on a feeling to serve because it is not, at least in that moment, in line with our priorities, that is okay. Generosity is about creating a better overall life by engaging in better habits. It is not about exhausting yourself with every possible opportunity. By the time you are done reading this book you will have the tools to be both efficient and impactful with your generosity.

Having a grateful disposition allows us to empathize, even in those situations when we don't act. We can allow ourselves to feel compassion even when we don't physically do anything, or as we are still thoughtfully considering the plea for service.

Each little act of generosity changes your heart.

One of the most important skills you will develop during your Generosity Experiment is learning the difference between "what it means to appear right" and "finding the right answer."

Wanting to appear right is a natural inclination for most of us. This is a tricky topic because having a sincere concern for an outcome *being* right and *appearing* right can seem to have very similar motives, but our need to appear right is the the primary food source for our egos. Without some safety nets, it is really hard to walk the line between being right and appearing right without allowing our ego to be fed. The ego is concerned with being important and mattering. The more we feed our own egos, the less importance we place on others and their perspectives. Feeding your ego will eventually leave you isolated on an island—you might be the most important person on that island, but you'll also be alone.

Our framework for what is "right" depends on what we know — in other words, what we have learned through culture, religion, parents, friends, and other past experiences. This process of learning what is and is not acceptable in society is called "socialization." Based largely on socialization, two people may have vastly different concepts of what is "right." But, if our mental frameworks are based on what we know, they are also based on what we don't know. We have many limitations to knowing the best and most correct answer in any given situation. What is "right" in our mind is often what we perceive as expected in our social circumstances.

These mental frameworks, known in psychology as "schemas," are helpful in that they allow us to assess and interpret the world quickly and efficiently. But, schemas can also be incredibly flawed and lead us to incorrect conclusions.

Sometimes it is easy to get caught in the no man's land between what we feel we should do and what society tells us is acceptable. What we feel we should do comes from within us. It does not matter if you call it intuition, spirit, or consciousness; the important distinction is that it comes from within. The expectation society places on us comes from without, imposed on us by our desire to stay within the boundaries that society has delineated.

Trying to decide between our own moral compass and society's expectations can be paralyzing. All too often we end up hiding behind what is socially acceptable in lieu of doing what we feel we should do. I found that too many times when I got caught in this position, I end up not taking action at all, and failing by both my own and society's standards.

Think of it this way: Have you ever been in an argument with someone and there comes a point when you realize that you might be wrong? You start to feel that you may not have had all the information needed to make the best and most efficient argument, It is at that point that you make a choice. You either acknowledge that you may have taken an incorrect stance, or you double down and continue to defend your side even though you know it's wrong. When we double down even when we know or even suspect that we are wrong, it is usually in an effort to appear right. It's an effort to save face, focused on self-esteem instead of on bettering the self or building relationships with others.

This was the usual argument in my head when I had opportunities to be generous. I would ask myself, "What is the right thing to do?"

"Is giving money the smartest thing?"

"Is giving money just enabling the person I am trying to help?"

Often that argument would last long enough for either the opportunity to be generous to pass or for me to rationalize my way out of it, because I couldn't come to the conclusion of how I could be right in a given situation!

The problem with our quest to appear right is that we compare our giving to what is expected, or to what other people do. It is perhaps easiest to see the multitude of expectations people have surrounding generosity when someone in the public eye is charitable. When someone famous gives, there is plenty of judgment about whether or not they made the right choice. Comments could be: "They didn't give the right amount," or "They didn't give locally," or "They picked the wrong cause," and on and on.

The interesting thing is, if that person hadn't given at all, no one would say a thing, and this is the route that is too often taken because of fear of criticism and not meeting expectation.

To me, being "right" had more to do with satisfying my pride than actually wanting to bring about the highest good. My pride wanted to make sure that what I did with my money was going to actually make a difference. I wanted to make sure that my time, my money, or any other capital that I would invest in being generous was going to be able to produce some good and not go to waste. We are sometimes so focused on the end result and what we think it should look and feel like, that we fail to act at all.

Approaching generosity with an "appearing right" attitude is much like being in an argument about what color the pearly gates are when you're standing right in front of them. You are focused on the wrong thing! Applying generosity this way won't create the result you want from your life or this experiment. In order to create more connection, more gratitude, and a more generous habit, we have to stop being so concerned with ourselves.

So, if the goal is not to appear right, then what is the goal?

We need to have guidelines to abide by. We need to have a new goal. What I didn't realize was that I already had that goal, but I was leading with the wrong part. I was leading with my ego and it was getting in the way of the journey.

The goal I had was not to give the smartest and most efficient way, it was about using generosity as way to become a better person. Living in harmony with our inner compass, we will often be prompted to do things that will go against the grain of appearing right. What if, instead of worrying about what is "appearing right," we instead focused on "finding the right answer"? Finding the right answer is about honoring the person you want to become in the future with the choices you make today.

Finding the right answer is harder because it always allows the opportunity to give something. What this requires, then, is for you to develop deeper generosity skills. It requires you to develop a generous disposition.

If I were to draw out a plan of how to best help the homeless, for example, it would probably not involve simply handing out money. I am a firm believer in teaching a man how to fish and feeding him for life rather than giving him a fish and feeding him for a day. But the first step might be giving him a fish, to sate his hunger in the present and to develop your awareness to a point where you can recognize which acts of generosity will serve someone with lasting effects.

It is easy to get caught up in judgement of how others will receive your generosity and what they will do with what is given to them. We should never let the possibility of someone else being dishonest or irresponsible prevent us from honoring the nature that is in us to give.

In cities across the world, people stand or sit on street corners with signs asking for help in some way. When I encountered this, rather than getting in my head and listing all the reasons why giving money directly to a homeless person is not smart or efficient, I reframed the exchange. Instead, when I had the impulse to give, I did, even if others may think it's not the best way to give. The point is to start the habit of giving, to put yourself on the path to becoming a giving person.

This was the start of a habit, and by reframing my thoughts I was able to serve the end that I had in mind for this experiment.

All too often, we forgo giving the fish for that day because it is better to teach that man how to fish. But then we never get around to doing either. So just give him the fish, change your heart, and someday perhaps you can teach him to fish. Take the first step to generosity now, and worry about perfecting that step in the future.

Once you overcome your skepticism and take the first step toward generosity, you may still find yourself encountering the skepticism of others. When you encounter negative reactions from others, it's important to remember that your generosity is yours to control, regardless of what others think.

I love this little allegory of a man not willing to sacrifice his generous nature:

A man and his friend had taken a camping trip, and were relaxing in front of a campfire. They suddenly saw a snake come out of the flames, wriggling in pain. The first man reached into the flames and pulled out the snake to save it. As he grabbed the snake, it bit his hand and, in a reflex, the man let go of the snake. As soon as the snake fell back into the fire, the man immediately reached back into the fire to pluck it out again. And again, the snake bit him. The man again shook the snake free, only to see it fall back into the fire. As the man started to reach out once again to pull the snake from the fire, his friend called out to him. "Don't be a fool for a third time," the friend said. "The snake has already bitten you twice, this third time it will only bite you again."

But the friend was surprised by the man's response. "Just because the nature of the snake is to bite me, that doesn't mean that I will alter my nature, which is to help," the man replied. With that, the man picked up a stick, using that to free the snake from the fire and from certain death.

The moral is simple: Don't allow the negative nature of some or all of those around you to change the positive nature that God has given you to share with all. There is nothing wrong with being smart about your generosity, as long as you continue to help, save, support, encourage, and strengthen those around you regardless of their actions or reactions. Focus more on your own character and less on the character of those you help and those who call out criticisms.

Imagine a staircase that leads to a generous disposition. The first step is awareness, and the second is taking opportunities to be generous, which then leads to a habit.

The purpose of my Generosity Experiment was to develop this new habit. I was not concerned with what was "right" or "the best possible way to give." If I saw an opportunity to be generous and took it. This perspective shift transformed my need to be generous to a need to find someone to receive that generosity.

Giving a homeless man a five dollar bill may be the right thing to do with what I know now. Maybe later on, I will learn a different and better way to be generous. But that perspective is really secondary to the act of giving. The key is to keep giving, learning, and growing.

The point of generosity is not to find solutions for people who have it worse off than you; it is about building up the human soul. Both the person who is generous, and the person who is the recipient of the generosity benefit from the experience. The more generous acts a person does, the more prepared their life will become to receiving generosity. In turn, that person will be able to develop a more generous disposition, and the people they are generous to are able to feel connection and love.

As your generosity increases, you will begin to see others in a new light. It will be much easier to stand in their shoes and love them right where they are.

The answer is not always to give no matter what the cost or the opportunity. As you develop a more generous heart, it will become a reflex for you to see not just a need, but a living, breathing person. Sometimes the most effective gift you can give is love.

In essence, the right answer is already within you. When you keep in mind the end goal to become a more generous person, you will find the right answer. When you do this first, then you can figure out what the best or "right" thing is to give to someone.

> #1 THE RIGHT ANSWER: Something that progresses you toward your end goal. A state of being, a direction.
>
> #2 APPEARING BEING RIGHT: Putting your need for self-importance above the end goal of what you are becoming.

In order to fully incorporate generosity into our lives and to take full advantage of the blessings it has to give, we have to lead with the pursuit to find the "right answer" and let go of "being right."

A large portion of the need I had to be right was rooted in expectations from both myself and from society. It was when I decided that I was going to make "yes" my default answer, that I started to realize how much I had said "no." The majority of times I said "no" was because of my need, in some way, to be right.

The 90/10 Rule

One of the biggest things holding me back from being more committed to generosity was inner conflict, something we all experience. It's like a war between giving as we have been accustomed to giving and allowing our giving to follow our intuition. The conflict can look very different depending on how generosity is defined by each of us as individuals .

The Habit

Dr. Maxwell Maltz wrote in his book *Psycho-Cybernetics* about the level to which our habits are ingrained into our lives.

"Our self-image and our habits go together," Maltz wrote. "Change one and you will automatically change the other."[4]

The word "habit" originally meant garment, or clothing. This gives us an insight into the true nature of habits. Our habits are literally something that we "put on." These habits are not accidental, we have them because they fit us. They are consistent with the self-image we have developed about ourselves. The good thing about habits is that they can be changed. This is a hopeful fact for someone who has created habits that are not serving them.

When it comes to generosity, we have all developed our own set of habits. Some of these habits aid us in our enjoyment of the blessings generosity has to offer, while other habits prevent us from living a more generous life.

Habits that we have developed when it comes to how we see people and how we give to others, are what I call the habit zone. Everyone will have a distinctly individual habit zone because it is based on our personal experience. We become attached to the habits we have created around generosity because we have been wearing most of them for so long. These habits have come to signal to the world what kind of person we are and how generous we can be.

Habits play a big role in the way our lives are affected by generosity. Something I learned throughout my Experiment was that the more I went outside of my habit zone and helped in ways that challenged the social norms that had shaped my habits, the more connected I felt to other people.

There are two places from which we give our generosity:

1. Comfort Zone Giving: Your 90%.

This is where 90 percent of our generosity opportunities come. During the course of our lives, each of us has been socialized to exhibit a certain baseline of generosity. For instance, you might think it is polite to hold doors open for others or that it's standard to pick up someone's wallet or phone if they drop it in front of you, and it might be almost automatic to smile and apologize if you accidentally bump into someone. We learn these habits from society. It is almost as if we have been assigned the role generosity is to play out in our lives, so it is second nature for us. Acting from the comfort zone is comfortable for us because we feel it's expected of us and we have grown accustomed to behaving in that way.

This type of giving has led us to think that we are generous even when we are really just giving within our comfort zone. Giving in the 90 percent is still good, but there is so much more out there for us. The dangerous part is that I—like so many others—was only somewhat generous, just "enough" to grab the title of a generous person. But this level of generosity is not quite enough to enjoy the blessings of connection, belonging, self worth, love, and perspective that I have been taught my whole life generosity can bring.

2. Miracle Living: Your 10%.

When we have a 10% experience we step outside of the norm, outside of what is expected. This might feel awkward at first because you are stepping outside of your comfort zone, but remember that your comfort zone can be expanded by continually pushing the limits.

There is a scene in the 1989 movie *Indiana Jones and the Last Crusade* where Indiana is trying to get to the holy grail so his father can be saved by drinking the everlasting waters. On his way to the grail there is a series of tests Indiana has to complete.

In this particular scene, Indiana comes to a cliff's edge and the map tells him that he needs to "leap from the lion's head to prove his worth." His first response to the test is, "This is impossible," because all he can see is the gulf that is between himself and the other side. He mutters under his breath "God's math," meaning that this was God's way of building him and proving him to be worthy of the prize he was seeking.

In true Indiana Jones fashion, he lifts his foot high up in the air and takes a step forward, landing safely on an invisible bridge that was there all along. As he continues across the bridge, the way becomes easier, the pathway reveals itself to him, and with each step Indiana gains more confidence.

Miracle living can feel much like what Indiana Jones felt on that bridge. You might feel a little crazy for acting on your sense to reach out and start a conversation with a stranger, but these are the moments to place your trust in what you can't see.

These moments are more rare than comfort-zone giving, and we see them about 10 percent of the time. When I'm taking part in these opportunities, it is then I start to comprehend "God's math." It is when I step into the 10 percent that I can see beyond expectation and become the exception. These types of opportunities increase our awareness that we need each other and we are meant to connect with each other.

When opportunities to push our generosity into the 10 percent arise, we may feel uncomfortable because it is not a place that we have spent much of our time. Most of us have been living up to expectations that either we have placed on ourselves, or that we have allowed others to place on us. But when we venture into the seldom-visited world of the 10 percent, we get a glimpse of something bigger than ourselves. When we take up residence there, we can start to see that other people are just like us. Our differences start to fade away and we can begin to feel connected instead of isolated and alone.

There will always be a 10 percent to push toward, but as we continue to take steps forward we will become more confident in our journey.

David McRaney explores the connection between our attitudes and actions in his book *You Can Beat Your Brain:*

"For many things, your attitudes came from actions that led to observations that led to explanations that led to beliefs. Your actions tend to chisel away at the raw marble of your persona, carving into being the self you experience from day to day. It doesn't feel that way, though. To conscious experience, it feels as if you were the one holding the chisel, motivated by existing thoughts and beliefs. It feels as though the person wearing your pants performed actions consistent with your established character, yet there is plenty of research suggesting otherwise. The things you do often create the things you believe."[5]

Generosity can only be cultivated in the brain for so long before it needs to become action. Each generous choice you make will deepen your understanding of the value of each individual.

One of the indicators I get that tells me that I am looking at a 10 percent opportunity is that I find myself in my head, trying to rationalize why it is okay to not give and instead giving myself the proverbial pat on the back. I tell myself I am still a good person, even if I don't do this (10 percent) thing, because I do all these other (90 percent) things.

You might find that you have different indicators that tell you when you have a 10 percent opportunity in front of you. It is not important that we have the same indicator, but it is paramount that you recognize what that indicator is and then create an action plan whenever you encounter a 10 percent opportunity. When you feel and recognize your personal indicators, that will be your crucial moment and the crucial time for you to act.

These 10 percent moments will appear more often the more you act on them, continually broadening your perspective. I like to think of these moments as invitations. Invitations to learn something, to make a connection, to grow your perspective, and to make a difference.

Your own 10 percent experiences, however, do not exist so that you can compare them with other people's 10 percent experiences. We all have a different 10 percent, and what might seem difficult for one person to do may seem easy for someone else. Remember, this is *your* experiment and is not a time for you to compare yourself with what other people are doing. If you find yourself having a hard time with this, please go back and re-read Chapter 2.

In addition to not comparing yourself to others, it is also important that you do not forgo your 90 percent in search of the 10 percent. You cannot have the 10 percent if you don't have a 90 percent. You need both to benefit 100% from generosity in your life.

Little vs. Big

You might find yourself having to constantly fight the urge to pass the seemingly little acts of generosity in anticipation for the big ones that, in my mind, had the potential to change someone's life.

Often when we think of being intentionally generous, our thoughts go to the things we see marketed to us that have usually been produced, funded, and organized by professionals. This includes large-scale campaigns such as those asking for donations to cure cancer or a trip to Disneyland planned by the Make-a-Wish Foundation. I am not suggesting that professionals who market generosity are bad, but it can give us unrealistic expectations of what generosity should look like. And, in fact, it can prevent us from receiving the benefit of the small opportunities that we have all around us.

Honor the small acts. They make up the majority of what you will experience with generosity. Those small opportunities are like the score to a good movie, they will be the soundtrack for your life. It is those small acts that put you in the place of highest potential. Those little things are what come together to make big things, and you won't need professional funding, camera crews, or elaborate planning—they will just happen.

We can never really tell what may be a "big" thing to someone else. Maybe a few dollars has the ability to make a difference or a loving conversation will save someone's life. Sometimes, a genuine, but small, act can have more impact than a prearranged big act.

There is no better way to cultivate gratitude for your own life than by giving other people a reason to be grateful for theirs. As you follow through on the tugs you feel on your heartstrings to be generous in small ways, it will astound you how grateful you are for the small things in your own life. It is about honoring the process and letting it take hold of your life.

Often when being generous, we are found battling the balance of how much it will matter and what will make a difference. Often when I see campaigns asking for money or when I see a homeless person on the street, I ask myself, "What is a few bucks going to do, really?"

Lottery winners have been well documented as not having any significant increase of happiness after their big paydays. This is because, when the primary benefactor of the money is ourselves, it is not typical to experience a significant increase in happiness level. But when we *give*, even in small amounts, for the benefit of others, it consistently rewards us with increased happiness.

Harvard professors Michael Norton and Elizabeth Dunn have done extensive research investigating the common saying "money can't buy happiness." They wanted to know if perhaps money *could* buy happiness. In one of the studies, they gave money to two groups of people. Organizers told the first group that they could only spend the money on themselves, and they told the other group they could only spend the money on others.

The organizers of the study called each of the participants to ask how they gave and if they felt an increased sense of happiness. Without fail, those who gave to others felt an increase in happiness while those that spent on themselves felt no difference.

The beauty of generosity is that it is not about the amount of money or goods that we give, it is about the process of directing our minds outside of ourselves.

Most of the time when we forgo a generous act, it is because of inward thoughts of inconvenience or insignificance. But just giving anything can break the cycle of inward thought and turn us toward the people that surround us instead of away from them.

Remember that this is meant to be YOUR Generosity Experiment. You get to define the rules. Ask yourself: what am I trying to prove? What do I want to create with my actions?

Chapter 3 Challenges:

- *Turn inward. What is in your heart that prevents you from reaching your full potential? Which of these things do you control, and which do other people control?*

- *Next time you have an opportunity to give, stop and consider whether it's a 10 percent or 90 percent moment. What factors do you look for to identify the 10 percent moments? What are you feeling or thinking? How can you start seeing more of these?*

- *List the small acts of generosity that you do every day. What can you do to honor these acts?*

Chapter 4
Cognitive Dissonance

Rationalization is the enemy of moral progress.
—Jonathan Haidt, American social psychologist

Defining Cognitive Dissonance

Most of us try our best to keep our thoughts, perceptions, and beliefs consistent with the choices we make throughout our lives. In today's constantly changing and diverse world, this is not always possible.

Cognitive dissonance is the discomfort and internal tension that arises when a person holds two conflicting beliefs in their mind at the same time, or acts in a way inconsistent with their beliefs. Feeling cognitive dissonance can make us feel like hypocrites.

What exactly causes cognitive dissonance and how it influences our behaviour is not always so clear.

In the late 1950s, social psychologists began to research this phenomenon. According to Leon Festinger, author of the book *A Theory of Cognitive Dissonance*, the important factor in cognitive dissonance theory is the principle of *cognitive consistency*. This principle says that we, as humans, will seek consistency in our beliefs and attitudes in any situation where two cognitions are inconsistent. Inconsistency of this sort causes psychological distress, and so we are motivated to reduce it—if the distress persists it can lead to depression and symptoms anxiety.

Festinger describes three relationships between our thoughts and our actions: a consonant relationship, an irrelevant relationship, and a dissonant relationship. A *consonant relationship* is when two cognitions or actions are consistent with each other, such as when you believe you are an honest person, and you tell the truth about a situation. An *irrelevant relationship* is when two cognitions or actions don't really have anything to do with each other, such as liking dogs and reading a book. A *dissonant relationship*, which is the focus of this chapter, is when two cognitions or actions conflict. For example, when you believe you are an honest person, yet you end up telling a lie, even if it's just a small white lie.

Because of the uncomfortable feeling brought on by the dissonant relationship, the person then tries to reduce the tension and psychological stress by trying to change their behavior or justify their conflicting cognition.

There are generally three ways that people commonly try to reduce their cognitive dissonance:

1. Changing the behavior or the cognition. For example, if a person smokes when he knows it is not good for him, he will quit smoking.

2. Justifying the cognition or behavior. The smoker tries to convince himself that smoking isn't that bad because he can't avoid every other health risk out there anyway. The smoker might try to tell themselves the likelihood of weight gain if they quit smoking, and therefore decide not to quit smoking in order to prevent the weight gain.

3. Ignoring or denying the information or action that conflicts with their beliefs or relevant current cognitions; this is the ostrich approach. The person may also actively avoid situations and information likely to increase the cognitive dissonance.

One famous example of cognitive dissonance is the fable of *The Fox and the Grapes*, by Aesop.[6]

This fox has a longing for grapes:
He jumps, but the bunch still escapes.

So he goes away sour;
And, 'tis said, to this hour
Declares that he's no taste for grapes

In the story, the fox sees high-hanging grapes and wants so badly to be able to eat them. However, once he comes to the conclusion that he cannot reach them, he then convinces himself that the grapes are likely unripe and sour. The moral of the story is that "a fool despises what he cannot get." The cognitive dissonance theory says that the fox diminished his cognitive dissonance by convincing himself that his object of desire was worthless, and adapted his thoughts to the situation. In other words, the fox chose option two: he justified his his desire to get the grapes to lessen the blow of wanting something he was not willing to keep trying to get.

The degree to which different people experience dissonance, or the lack of harmony between their thoughts and actions, depends on a few different factors.

In my case, I experienced the most cognitive dissonance around my self image, and it took my undertaking this experiment to realize it.

I became aware of a lack of harmony between whom I believed myself to be and my actions. This dissonant relationship was very alarming to me. I had not realized that, in order to relieve the discomfort of acting in a way that conflicted with my self-image, I had rationalized my thoughts and actions.

Out of the four ways to reduce the discomfort of cognitive dissonance—in my case, not being the person I wanted to see myself as—the most difficult, but ultimately best, is option one: changing the behavior or cognition. Which for me, meant actually becoming the person, through action, that I believed I was (or should have been). It meant taking an honest look at where I fell short, owning it, and then making choices that honored the person I hoped to be.

And finally, overcoming my cognitive dissonance meant having to take a look at the excuses that had become so habitual that they were second nature to me. These excuses are the one that will always came to our rescue whenever we began to feel the slightest discomfort from the thought that our actions were not living up to the image we have of ourself.

The foremost facet of this self-image was that I was a generous person. I felt driven to be generous in my speech, my actions, and even my private thoughts and feelings. But here's the problem. The choices I was making in each of those areas were far from the generous ideal I had envisioned. I was betraying my own motivations with every move I made. In order to uphold the belief I had about who I was, I had to make a choice. Either change my behavior and become the person I wanted to be and enjoy the blessing I knew would follow, or take the easy route and tell the little voice inside me to shut up.

After a while your subconscious gets so loud that it becomes impossible to ignore. As I soon discovered, that little voice will not be quieted. And if you continue to pretend you don't feel cognitive dissonance, it will slowly overtake your life. You'll shy away from choice to avoid thinking too hard, and soon you're well on your way down an unintentional path that only leads farther and farther away from the fulfilled life you could have had. It is not that you chose to be unfulfilled, but to get off that path, you have to be proactive.

Dealing with Dissonance

Remember the three main ways people reduce the discomfort surrounding cognitive dissonance? My own experience has taught me that there are a few more sneaky ways we circumvent our cognitive dissonance.. Read on to check yourself against these avoidance techniques that might prevent you from overcoming your dissonance.

Imagine a shelf in your house. All the blessings that come from acting on your generosity are stacked on the shelf. At the bottom you have the basic blessings, those received from the easiest acts of generosity, the next row is made up of the more impressive blessings, and so on. You can only benefit from the blessings you can reach. If you want to reach the higher blessings you have to build a ladder to help you tap into your generous spirit and reach those higher shelves. It WILL NOT just appear. This chapter in particular, will provide you with an essential step you'll need on your climb to the top shelf.

1. Compartmentalization: Our Hidden Boxes

"Compartmentalization" is an unconscious psychological defense mechanism used to avoid cognitive dissonance.

In layman's terms, compartmentalization is putting something into a mental "box" of sorts in order to protect ourselves from the truth.

There is a high probability that you are compartmentalizing and don't even realize it. Because our minds are programmed to mediate any cognitive dissonance, they do it automatically, without us paying much attention. Unfortunately, compartmentalizing can have negative consequences; most importantly, it may cause us to miss out on the benefits we would enjoy if we *didn't* ignore the truth, if we didn't avoid the dissonance.

For example, consider gossip. Most of us would agree with Benjamin Franklin when he said:

"I resolve to speak ill of no man whatever, not even in a matter of truth; but rather by some means excuse the faults I hear charged upon others, and upon proper occasions speak all the good I know of everybody."[7]

We agree with Benjamin Franklin because we understand the damaging and morally corrosive effects of gossip. Gossip is a clever vice, and it is easy to get caught off guard when it seems to sneak up on us. I have made a commitment to myself to avoid gossip and when possible, stop it. However, the conversations that always seem to catch me off guard are those about politics. It seems as though most conversations about politics turn into conversations about people.

Because I'm trying to honor my commitment to eradicate gossip from my life, I'm hyper aware of it, so I am very aware of the uneasy feeling I get when the conversation turns from talking about policy to talking about people. At this point I have a few choices: One, walk away or stop it, or two, ease my discomfort and tell myself that this politician chose to be in the public eye and therefore what I say about him or her won't qualify as gossip. In other words, I'd compartmentalize my feelings about gossip, making an exception for myself for this situation. If I choose to rationalize why it is okay to gossip, it doesn't matter how good the excuse is, I will not be able to escape the ugly consequences of gossip.

Gossip is not the only area of life compartmentalization can have damaging effects. I found that I had become very comfortable with the contradiction I was living when it came to generosity. As part of humanity, we intuitively know to some extent what generosity is at its core. When our actions don't line up with our belief system, in order to live with ourselves, we place our exceptions neatly in a box, wrap them with rationalization and compartmentalize. We say things like, "Yes I believe we should always tell the truth *except* in this situation" or "I believe we should forgive everyone *except* for this type of person." You cannot make up your own rules when it comes to principles, and compartmentalizing your exceptions will only disguise the real problem.

We may feel that ignoring the boxes we've stowed away works, but this kind of path leads to frustration, to constant wondering why we don't enjoy the full measure of generosity (or of any virtue for that matter).

Anytime we betray our sense of goodness, when we hold out on things like love, gratitude, forgiveness, generosity, compassion, and empathy, not only are we choosing a life full of cognitive dissonance, we create a fissure between the virtue and our ability to enjoy its blessing.

There will be times when it is not possible to give, or when it is possible, but you don't feel it is right—and that's okay. Your generous spirit rises before the gift is even given. Simply seeing someone as worthy of love and respect is the first step toward a generous life and the key to giving with pure motivations.

It can be a scary thing to know that we are who we are because that is what we are *choosing*. It's scary to acknowledge that how we experience life is up to us. It is in this space that we can finally fully accept ourselves.

I remember one night in particular when I acted in contradiction to my beliefs about generosity. My wife and I had just come back from a dinner and movie date. The next day I had to be up early and be at my best to give an important presentation at work, so when we got home I paid the babysitter and scurried off to bed—not paying much attention to the mess that had been left by our children while we were gone. While I was lying in bed, I could hear my wife moving things here and there, cleaning up the messes that our kids had made.

As I was lying there listening, I had an urge get up out of bed and help her, to be giving with my time. I quickly shut that idea out of my mind, but in order to fall asleep, I had to do some mental gymnastics to make sure I didn't feel guilty for not helping. I had to compartmentalize and rationalize.

The first rationalization was that she was trying to guilt me into helping her by making so much noise. With this accusation, she became a manipulative wife not worthy of help.

When this idea didn't stick, the next rationalization was that she was a selfish person, and she needed to be taught a lesson, to take on some of the chores herself for a change.

Then came the thought that she was not considerate. Didn't she care that I had to be up early to provide for our family?

All the while, my wife had said nothing to me, but I had not only rationalized away my choice to not help, I did it by painting my wife as *unworthy* of the help. In twenty minutes, I had gone from a nice date with my wife to seeing her as the perpetrator and myself as the victim, all because I betrayed my sense of generosity.

This is what I did with the homeless man at the freeway off ramp that I mentioned earlier in this book. Because I chose not to follow through with what I felt I should do, I had to justify my reasons for not following through. In my mind, I found a way to not just make him unworthy of my generosity but also pat myself on the back for not being generous. I told myself that I was preventing him from feeding the addiction he must have had.

Cognitive dissonance leads to compartmentalization, rationalization, and justification. We create conflict where none need to exist. When we compartmentalize our actions and try to serve two different sets of rules it is living in contradiction.

2. Justification: The Stories We Tell Ourselves

Even though we may consider honesty to be a necessary virtue and important for us to strive toward, we find it easy to justify small white lies to people in our lives. We think, "Well, it is in everybody's best interest if I just lie this one time or about this one thing or to this one person." This allows us to tell ourselves the story that our dishonesty wasn't really our fault, it was necessary. In this way, we can believe we are not only honest but a good person who looks out for the best interest of others. we rationalize our dissonance away. But, as we are not truly living an honest lifestyle, we can't reap the full blessings from it, and our happiness and sense of purpose suffer.

Because we get so good at compartmentalizing and rationalizing our choices, we began to write new narratives for our lives. The new stories might feel "good" to us because we have neatly justified each opposing conflict. Unfortunately, when we justify ourselves out of practicing virtues like generosity, gratitude, or forgiveness even if it's just occasionally, we contradict the whole virtue and any notions we have of our identities in relation to it. Regardless of how well I justify withholding forgiveness from someone who I think is not deserving, I am still going against my beliefs about forgiveness and therefore cannot benefit from the full spectrum of the virtue. The new story we concocted is not, after all, as good for us as we thought.

Our journey to living a life that truly practices the virtues we value, in every situation, is ongoing. If we consistently evaluate how we are doing with a particular virtue, we make informed choices, leading to a reduction in cognitive dissonance and, ultimately, greater happiness.

Often, we inherently know how a virtue is uniquely designed to benefit our individual lives. So those times when you are prompted to do something that you know is "right" but fail to act is a form of self-betrayal. Acting contrary to how we feel will leave us scrambling to justify our choice. Justification only occurs when something doesn't feel quite right. If we were acting in alignment with how we feel, there would be no need to justify anything. But sometimes, we justify our behavior so automatically, we don't even realize it.

A few years ago, I was on a trip and it had been a long day of meetings and work. I was eager to get checked into my hotel, take a shower, and go to bed. As I was waiting in line to check in, there was a mother with a few older kids who were doing what any kids would do when it is late in the evening and they're being told to stand still in line at a hotel—they were bouncing around, pushing and teasing each other as they waited in line.

The family and I were both called up to the front desk at about the same time. When I was finished with the paperwork, the receptionist directed me to the elevators that would take me to my room on the third floor. On my way to the elevator, I noticed that as the lady with kids was finishing up the receptionist was pointing her to the same elevator I was just stepping onto. As I entered the elevator, I heard her say to one of her children, "Run ahead and hold the elevator."

In the elevator, there were two buttons—one to make the doors remain open and one to make the doors close faster. As I heard the mother tell her child to hold the elevator, instead of doing what I knew I should and press the first button, my finger went directly to the close door button. In fact, I think I might have hit it more than once. Just as the door was closing and it was too late for someone to stop it, I saw the kid through the closing door. I was struck with the thought that I had just betrayed my belief in generosity—I should have held the door.

You can probably imagine the justification I had to invent to make this choice okay. I had to puff myself up, telling myself that it was more important for me to ride that elevator alone, because I needed rest!

What I had done that day was more important than whatever the mother or those kids had done! Who brings kids to a hotel this late, anyway?

Then, I told myself that maybe it was in their best interest to ride an elevator without a stranger; with such unruly kids the mother was bound to feel less stressed if they had an elevator to themselves.

These were the stories I was telling myself to lessen the discomfort I felt by not acting in the way that I knew I should have. I knew the right thing, but I didn't do it. This was a classic case of cognitive dissonance. I then proceeded to make more wrong choices by attempting to ease the distress though justifying what I had done, rather than owning up to it and resolve to make a different choice next time. I had to tell myself a story that painted my actions in a way that allowed me to still believe myself a good person who had acted justly.

What I should have done was held the elevator, welcomed that family in, and helped them to their floor. I could have smiled at them, helped the mom feel less stressed, and been funny to the kids so they would have calmed down. It wouldn't have taken any more time, and it would have lightened everyone's mood. I could have been generous. I missed out on the good feeling that would have come from it, not to mention I would have avoided the distress caused by the dissonance

Many times when we justify our circumstances, we see the person who provided the potential opportunity as a mere object to use to justify our actions. When we fail to see them as a *person* like us, we lose the opportunity to connect. No matter how I tried to convince myself that what I did was okay, I betrayed the sense that I had to help.

Choosing Dissonance: A Life of Contradiction

The best, and in fact only, way to remedy cognitive dissonance for good is to face it and *change our behavior* to be in line with our beliefs. But if we still decide instead to simply, live with the dissonance, what will follow is an unhappy life built on contradiction.

In music, consonance is associated with sweetness, pleasantness and acceptability, while dissonance is associated with harshness, unpleasantness, or unacceptability. An unstable tone combination is a dissonance; its tension demands an onward motion to a stable chord. Thus dissonant chords are "active"; traditionally they have been considered harsh, expressing pain, grief, and conflict.

Just as it is with music, tension put on two opposing chords cannot be sustained. In our lives, it is the same. Our onward focus cannot be split among two conflicting values—just as it is with musical dissonance, it will only bring pain, grief, and conflict into our lives.

We may think, "I must be doing something wrong," or "There must be something wrong with me." And we may have no idea what is "wrong." But there is hope. If we choose to *stop accepting contradiction* in our lives, we become the ones in control. We can change the feelings of hopelessness to ones of empowerment and hope.

Overcoming Dissonance

If we don't keep ourselves in check, pretty soon cognitive dissonance becomes commonplace in our lives. We go from compartmentalizing or over-justifying to living an entire life of contradiction. And then we wonder why we are not happy.

We tell ourselves *I am grateful, I am forgiving, I am generous*, but we are not acting that way. We pick and choose when to be grateful, forgiving, generous, etc., effectively making their benefit to us a moot point.

How do we get past this? The first step is to notice cognitive dissonance when it arises. When we feel the stress of believing one way and wanting to act another way, instead of justifying or compartmentalizing it, we must recognize it, then choose to take charge by eliminating the conflicting behavior.

Although cognitive dissonance may put us into situations where compartmentalization or justification feel like the most comfortable choices (or even not like a choice at all), there are some things we can do to recognize the signs that we are hiding from cognitive dissonance, rather than fully eliminating it.

Some common indicators that we are experiencing cognitive dissonance are:

- **Feeling the need to justify**—You do not have to justify something that is not crooked in the first place.

- **Defensiveness**—We don't feel as compelled to defend our actions when they are aligned with our moral compass.

- **Blaming**—Blaming is a symptom of someone avoiding accountability for themselves.

- **Feeling victimized**—Feeling this way is the validation we use to rationalize blaming.

- **Putting labels on others**—When we label others it makes it easy to place blame and justify to explain our own discomfort.

- **Exaggeration**—This helps to justify our excuses.

Ultimately, these red flags arise when we are focused on ourselves, especially our temporary comfort. When we choose to act in line with what we know to be true, there is no need to employ any of the above indicators. Recognizing cognitive dissonance is is a big step toward living a life of true generosity.

Chapter 4 Challenges:

- *Identify what you want to feel more of in your life (Love, Gratitude, Generosity, etc.).*

- *Identify where you have compartmentalized and justified. Think back over the last week. Were there any specific circumstances where you justified or compartmentalized a behavior?*

- *Where is your cognitive dissonance? Using the list of indicators of the previous page, identify where you haven't addressed your cognitive dissonance.*

Chapter 5
The Pity Trap

Our human compassion binds us the one to the other—not in pity or patronizingly, but as human beings who have learnt how to turn our common suffering into hope for the future. —Nelson Mandela

The scene begins; A young African girl stands in an empty field. The camera is angled just slightly above her. Alone in an unnamed, unidentifiable place, the girl's head is turned to avoid being seen directly by those viewing her through their television sets.

The voiceover on the video starts: "This is Kali. She is seven. Her body is racked with pain from diseases; the same kind that killed her sister. If Kali goes without help, she could be next."

The scene shifts and now Kali sits in the empty doorway of the makeshift hut without a door that she lives in, looking down. As the camera pans closer to Kali, a single tear trickles down her face.

Sound familiar? This is the kind of advertising we have grown up seeing here in America. Whether it's a television commercial, magazine advertisement, or a billboard, they each have the same intent: to make you feel guilty enough to pull out your wallet and give.

When you visualize the commercial described above (or when you see a commercial like it), what does it illicit in you? If you had to pick one emotion to describe how you feel, which one would you use?

This kind of advertising has received a lot of criticism and has been labeled as "poverty porn" because it's exploitative of the people they're trying to help. It's misleading and it perpetuates a stigma about poor communities in Africa. Yet, some argue that as long as these advertising strategies raise the money or generate aid to help people, why does it matter how ethical we view them to be?

The Australian Council for International Development (ACFID), which represents 135 organizations internationally, has created a code of conduct for advertisers, prohibiting this type of advertising, as it does not provide the best outcome for anyone involved.

Marc Purcell of the ACFID said that the code's purpose is to "ensure a respectful and truthful portrayal of the local people involved in developmental and aid activities….The code suggests not using images that manipulate a story to portray people in a pitiful way and to ensure they 'honestly convey the context and complexity of the situations in which local people live.'"[8]

Commercials like these are easy to spot, but because there's such a steady barrage of them, we have become conditioned to see less fortunate people in our daily lives through a pitiful lens. It is impossible to see honestly when our eyes are full of pity. The people pictured in advertisements or even someone we pass on the street are more than the struggles they face. When we see people as objects to be pitied, we strip people of the dignity they deserve, and we lose the ability to see them as they are.

I like to think of these "poverty porn" commercials as the some most obvious examples of a "Pity Trap"—those situations or habits that drag us down into pity, preventing us from being truly generous. But there are other, harder-to-spot traps all around us and inside us. This chapter will discuss three other Pity Traps that are hidden in plain site.

A Disdainful Distance

The first pity trap is that *pity* is, inherently, about helping "them"—that is, someone that seems different from you, who seems to be valued differently, whom you perceive to deserve more or less than yourself or others.

Whereas, *compassion* is about recognizing there is no such thing as "them." Compassion, if we break down the word to its Latin origin, is: 'com' which means to be with, 'passion' which means to endure, undergo, experience. So, quite literally, to have compassion for someone is to have a shared experience with another person.

Pity and compassion are very close in their meanings much like blame and accountability like we discussed in chapter 2. In essence, they both involve your feelings toward someone who is experiencing a hardship. The difference is your *attitude* toward this person, and the proximity to which you stand in relation to them—are you viewing them from a disdainful distance, from a position of superiority, or do you see them as right on your level?

Pity is the sorrow caused by the suffering and misfortunes of others. When generosity is at its highest potential in your life, it is void of sorrow.

There is a misconception that generosity is given to those that *need* by those that *have*. And if we didn't label people as either needy or privileged, than this definition might be okay. But when we sort our entire identities into categories like needy and privileged, or middle class and poor, we are giving ourselves guidelines on who deserves pity and therefore generosity.

The reality is that we are all needy, and we all have something to offer, regardless of the zip code or country in which we live.

On the TED stage, motivational speaker Ash Beckham talked about how hard is not relative: "HARD IS JUST HARD."[9] You cannot compare your hard to someone else's hard. Trying to compare bankruptcy to cancer to a five-year-old losing their parent is impossible. Hard is just hard, and it requires empathy to see everybody you meet as a complex person who has something to offer and who probably also has some form of hard in their life.

You might ask: What is wrong with feeling sorry for somebody in a particularly difficult situation?

When we pity, we feel bad that someone is going through something, but at the same time, we view the object of our pity as lesser than us, at least in that circumstance. Because of this, pity works against us when we are trying to do anything good.

When we pity someone, or feel sorry for them, we assume their situation isn't worthy of their gratitude. We think, *How could they possibly feel grateful for anything in the situation they're in?* But an essential truth of gratitude is the belief that something good can be derived from anything. Therefore, if your goal is to live a life of gratitude, pity just doesn't fit. Instead of pitying someone, you should see them as able to learn something from whatever situation they're in (and you able to learn from them!).

Pity Turned Inward

If we believe that some people deserve pity, then we also subscribe to the idea that *we* are entitled to a certain amount of pity from those whom we view as "more privileged" than us. The consequence of such a view is that the further down the ladder you see yourself, the less inclined you are to share what you have to offer, and the more likely you are to expect generosity from others.

Self-pity is perhaps the worst pity trap of all, because as soon as we see ourselves as worthy of our own pity, it becomes increasingly impossible to learn from our circumstances and improve our life. It is also impossible to hold gratitude and pity in your mind at the same time for very long—eventually one will win. Helen Keller said, "self-pity is our worst enemy and if we yield to it, we will never do anything wise in the world."

When we carry self-pity, it makes us feel terrible. Feeling sorry for ourselves will not provide us with a productive outcome. We are the controller of our destiny, the stewards over our lives. Self-pity means we are giving up that authority. Self-pity means we are focused only on ourselves and, moreover, focused on the negative.

And yet, even in the throes of self-pity, we still turn around and pity other people. In those moments, we feel benevolent in pitying someone else, because we have shifted our focus briefly from our own negative situations to someone else's.

It is a double standard, but so many of us get stuck in that trap. We are okay with giving help, but not okay receiving help.

The Tetris Effect

The Tetris Effect (also known as the Tetris Syndrome) happens when someone devotes such a long time and attention to an activity that it begins to pattern their thoughts and mental images. Its nickname comes from the video game Tetris.

If you have played Tetris enough over an extended period of time, you have probably experienced this phenomenon. You might take a walk around the neighborhood and see all sorts of shapes—houses, cars—that would fit together like Tetris blocks.

> Sea legs are another form of the Tetris effect. A person who has spent long periods at sea has a hard time not swaying back and forth when they are back on land.

This effect has powerful implications in our lives; when we become used to seeing things a certain way, we tend to look for those same things in our day-to-day reality. And when it comes to pity, the Tetris Effect is huge: it's the third Pity Trap.

Most of us grew up in a culture where pity was leveraged against us, often in the form of the aforementioned "poverty porn," as a way to elicit our charity. This conditioned pity works just like the Tetris effect. Often, just as it is when we are taking a stroll after playing Tetris and we see natural objects fitting together like blocks, we experience the same thing with pity. We are using the same old patterns that have been programmed in our subconscious to pity those that appear to be worse off than us. We almost feel guilty for not pitying them. It is how our minds have been trained.

What I Learned From Pity

When I went to Africa, although I didn't realize it at the time, I was seeing the residents of towns I visited in the way I had been conditioned to see them—with pity.

My first day in Ghana was spent in the city of Accra, and then we were to travel out to the village where we would spend the majority of our time.

That first night, I wanted to go out and experience Accra at night. As I approached the beach I could see the shops that lined the road. Further down, there was a man standing alone on the street outside one of the stores; I noticed him and he noticed me. The closer I got to the shops the more apparent it was that I was not going to be able to avoid a conversation with him. Being a student of sales and priding myself on being able to sniff out tactics used to part me from my money, my sleazy-salesperson-sensors were on high alert. So when this man approached me and was nice, interested, and polite, instead of seeing him for what he was, I put up walls. After all, I was not there to "be served," I was there to "serve them."

Nevertheless, the man and his friend invited me to come look at their shop. They played a spectacular five minute drums concert for us in front of their shop, and we bought a few things. At first, this didn't feel comfortable to me. I was not very accepting of their generosity; it wasn't because they weren't offering something sincere, it was because I had pity, pity not just for this man but for the entire people of Ghana.

As long as I had those feelings, I was prevented from sincerely receiving any generosity, let alone being generous myself.

So, imagine my surprise when the man, William, asked me if I wanted a tour of the area.

When I was unable to come up with a polite way to say no, I agreed to go with him. He took me to a little shanty town on the beach and introduced us to people. He had become the tour guide for the evening, offering historical knowledge, conversation, and a killer tour. Finally, we arrived back at the road on which we had first met. We exchanged information and said goodbye.

It was not until we had gone our separate ways that I realized—*wow, that was pretty special!* William had taken two hours out of his day away from his shop to spend time with me, helping me, becoming friends. In the moment I failed to see the generosity that was being offered to me. Because I was there to serve THEM, because I thought *I* had more to give *them*, I was not open to the thought that they had something different, but every bit as valuable, to offer me.

One of my biggest takeaways from my time with the people in those small villages in Africa was that happiness is a choice. When I pitied them, I couldn't see them clearly. I saw them as not having what I thought were the necessary components of happiness. Therefore, it was my misguided mission to give them that.

My ten days in Africa reminded me that happiness is a choice and that because of their circumstances, these people were afforded a very different perspective than what I was used to. It wasn't better or worse, it was just different. Until I was able to see them as my *partners* in generosity, I could not learn from them or their circumstances.

Our experiences give us the education we need to fulfill our purposes in life. We have all been given different circumstances so that as we work together as partners we can increase our happiness together. The key is to be open to new experiences that give us that chance.

Compassion, an Equal Partnership

The Dalai Lama once said, "Compassion is a necessity, not a luxury…it is a question of human survival." Compassion is the process of connecting by identifying with another person. Compassion can lead to increased motivation to do something in an effort to relieve the suffering of others. It is the antidote to any Pity Trap.

Real compassion gives us the opportunity to gain an education by immersion. Compassion encourages real empathy and allows us to not merely observe the suffering of someone, but to internalize their struggle. It has the power to make us aware of the learning opportunities both from the person we have compassion for and their circumstance.

Pity sees a problem to solve. Compassion sees a person to love and a circumstance from which to learn.

We can learn so many valuable lessons from people, especially from those who perhaps live a very different life than us. Can you imagine if we took the time to learn from one another, from our unique perspectives? The answers and solutions we would find would far surpass whatever strategies all the governments of the world could possibly devise.

> *"Pity and friendship are two passions incompatible with each other."*
> *—Oliver Goldsmith*

Generosity is not meant to be exclusively *given*; it is not a one-sided act. If we approach generosity viewing everyone around us as an equal partner, then as we offer help to some, we also see those same people as bringing something for us to the table. In order to be in an equal partnership, you have to see the person across from you as capable of offering generosity to you as you are to them. Having a generous disposition will allow you to hold even the negative reactions up as worthy of your gratitude. Life has a way of giving us the feedback we need to be our happiest selves.

The Latin root of the word "friend" means to love. In English, the meaning of friendship is to have a mutual affection or bond with someone. So, a friendship requires both parties to give love and both to receive love, otherwise it would not be considered a friendship.

Generosity works the same way. For generosity to work, just as in a friendship, both people in the "generosity" relationship are giving and both are receiving. Sometimes, just the very act of receiving a generous act is a gift in and of itself, but often there is much more to it.

When we approach a situation with an affection and respect for other people, it allows us to learn lessons that would not otherwise be present. It is like when you put your glasses on in a 3D movie and an entirely new experience unfolds.

Recently, my family and I went on a service trip to Mexico. One day, we volunteered at a charity that served breakfast and lunch in a small area near Tijuana. This little city was built on top of a landfill. This was not reclaimed land, redesigned for a neighborhood to be built. Instead, there was just a thin layer of dirt thrown on top of the massive hills of refuse that these homes had been created on.

On both sides of the mound were valleys, were retaining walls made of tires holding up the houses. Many of the dwellings were built out of whatever they could make use of from the ground beneath them.

At the local community building, we helped serve breakfast to the locals. Some of the kids had school uniforms on, other adults were dressed for work. Many of the people ate and went on their way. We were able to spend significant time with some people, including a young woman from the United states, who had been in charge of helping serve the people for the past three years.

When one of the volunteers from our group asked her, "When you look around and you still see so much 'need,' do you feel like you are making a difference?" Those of us from developed countries looked around and saw a huge problem. We see them as people "not like us." We saw them through the eyes of pity.

But this young woman offered another perspective—of compassion. She said, "You know what is amazing? We come here and see the poverty, and we want to fix it. We want to step in and make it the way we think it should be, to our standard of living.

"We don't *see* the people. We need to ask God what He thinks they need. God doesn't have pity on people. He sees the purpose in everything we go through. They can still have an immense amount of happiness and joy."

That was a learning experience for me. You are developing as a person, and as you have these experiences you are seeing others as worthy of giving and of love..

The best way to receive generosity is to give it.

Maybe until now you were a little like me before my Experiment. You felt that giving generosity should look like X. And receiving generosity should look like Y. But who says it has to be giving money? Or helping someone on the side of the road? Have you ever thought that you could be generous by saying no to someone?

There isn't one particular way that compassion looks. The difference is how you *see* the other person…as an object or as a person. Only when you see them as a person can you truly connect through generosity.

The Opportunity

I am sure you have heard of the term "hindsight is 20/20." Usually this phrase is used when we are trying to describe a difference in perspective; how in looking back we can see how a choice was either helpful or damaging, and we can at least view clearly the information gained or lesson learned from the experience. The more difficult the situations are, the more challenging it can be to gain the new, positive perspective. But that does not mean that it does not exist.

Hindsight is great, but I want to talk about having 20/20 vision *right now*. I don't like having to wait months, years, or even a lifetime to learn the lessons I need to learn to live a more happy and prosperous life. Seeing with 20/20 vision now can allow you to not only learn from your own experiences, it can also assist you in learning from others' difficulties and allow you to be an immediate, positive support for them in a trying circumstance.

When I was younger, before I was married, I had a married friend who had a disabled child. I had developed a certain amount of pity for him and his wife because I didn't take the time to understand their situation. Over the next years my sorrow resulted in us growing further and further apart I saw him as a victim and someone to be pitied. I found it hard to build a real relationship with him because I thought, "What could I offer someone with such a tremendous burden?"

Pity sometimes is our way out; it is how we cope with the hard circumstances of someone else. Frequently we get the opportunity to hear from people who have gone through hard things and we hear them recount lessons learned and changed perspective. But I missed that opportunity with my friend because I let his circumstance define him to me.

I reflect often on how life might be different if I had seen his trial as an *opportunity*, not just for him, but for me too. If only I would have approached it as a situation worthy of gratitude. Instead of shrinking, I could have leaned in to the friendship and offered a fresh perspective. The last thing we want to do in a hard situation is promote victimhood.

Choosing compassion in lieu of pity requires a mindset, and it also requires engagement. Don't be afraid to engage. It will open the door and allow you to see people with new eyes.

Chapter 5 Challenges:

- *Consider how pity could be hurting you. How is it preventing you from fully embracing the people that enter your life?*

- *Reread this chapter with your own attitude in mind and determine which Pity Traps you have fallen into. How can you begin to climb out?*

- *Try to shift your lens of pity to a lens of compassion. Who have you spent time with recently that you saw with pity? Rethink how you viewed them and translate your pity into compassion.*

Chapter 6
The Perfect Lie

It's hard to practice compassion when we're struggling with our authenticity or when our own worthiness is off-balance.
— Brené Brown, scholar, author, and public speaker

Social media gives us absolute control over what people are allowed to see. It has created a culture of perfection. Not perfect in the sense that it is without blemish, but in that we tend to display only what we feel are "accepted" imperfections or shortcomings.

In our personal "reality shows" we present to the world, we want people to see that we have it all together. Technology allows us the ability to pick and choose down to the smallest detail how our lives are portrayed to the world.

Although our increasingly digitized world may facilitate the the *perception of perfection* in new ways, this phenomenon is not a new one. Throughout history, the human race has always tried to convey strength, whether it be in battle, the boardroom, or a job interview. The last thing we want people to know is that we are flawed, because those flaws, we are told, present as weakness to the competition and will be exploited.

Instead of being forthright and leading with the things that truly make us like everyone else—our flaws—we hide them, and we hide *from* them. We obtain our short term goals, to seem strong and invinceable, essentially trying to please everyone else. Meanwhile we sacrifice our ultimate goal of happiness, joy, and connection.

We are living the Perfect Lie.

Maybe we have bought into the Perfect Lie because we feel the need to portray ourselves as perfect to hide our insecurities, or we assume that those we are comparing ourselves against *are* perfect. Really, it doesn't matter which one of these we start with; if we entertain either long enough, pretty soon we will be dealing with the damning influences of both of them.

Seeing someone else as perfect is a lie! Not only is it a lie, but it is the antithesis of the reason we are here on this earth. We were designed to fail, to have shortcomings, to be imperfect, and ultimately to learn from our mistakes by sharing them with each other. The Perfect Lie prevents us from this most basic form of generosity—that is, the willingness to be vulnerable, to care, in order to connect with someone else.

We seem to have an unspoken pact that we will not acknowledge anyone's need for generosity—except for when it's deemed acceptable. It's like when children (or adults for that matter) can see that they have both done something that would get them in trouble, and they say to each other, "I won't tell if you don't." When we acknowledge that we need help, it is an admission that we are not perfect, that we are broken in some way. It shatters the facade of perfection we have put up.

There are many ways we can be generous, ranging from giving from a distance, without vulnerability, to truly giving *for* another person. The latter involves us connecting personally with someone else; it requires a lowering of the boundaries we have put up, and it's a richer experience for both the giver and receiver. I realize there's a lot that happens in between these two sides of the spectrum—in fact, that is where most generosity takes place! Regardless of where we start out on the generosity spectrum, we should all aim for the generosity that mandates vulnerability. The deeper we venture inside another person's life, the more barriers we find but it is worth the effort..

It is easy for most of us to be generous with things that have become the social norm, but when it comes to asking a stranger how their day was and actually caring about the answer, we start to feel a little awkward, and we might even get some weird looks. Giving generously in this way makes us vulnerable, and vulnerability can make us feel uncomfortable when we want safe and protected.

Forging Intimacy

Most of the socially accepted forms of generosity honor the "I won't tell if you don't" contract. This is why you might get awkward looks as you dig in and ask deeper, more important questions.

Have you ever asked someone how their day was and received a response that went something like this: "Not very good, I haven't felt very well today"? Most of us have. If you are like most people, you may respond: "Oh, that's too bad. I hope your day gets better." But we're probably thinking, "I can't believe they took me literally, do they think I have time to hear how their day is actually going?" Then we get out of there as soon as we can to avoid hearing the drama of their life.

Being genuinely interested in someone is a higher level of generosity than the polite, cursory inquiries into their well-being, and it requires more from both the giver and the receiver. Most interactions fall short of deep connection in favor of the easier, quicker, accepted form of transactional generosity.

If you have ever been in a conversation where someone wants to share deeply, and you start to feel uncomfortable, it is probably because they are allowing you to see what is inside of them. They are sharing their vulnerabilities. It interrupts the way you are used to doing things.

I have always loved the play on the word *intimacy*: INTO-ME-YOU-SEE. Intimacy brings closeness, and what better way to create a connection than to share that which makes you the same? That is, your flaws.

When one person is sharing deeply with another, it is natural for the listener to feel responsible to share deeply as well. We are built this way. Humans were made for connection, and reciprocity is a fundamental way to build it. If you have ever been in a situation where both people or even a group of people share intimately, you will know the sense of connection you feel with those people, even if you've just barely met them.

Once I was asked what I did for work, and I gave the canned answer that I was accustomed to giving people I assumed didn't really care about what I said. But this time, the follow up question caught me off guard: "Does that make you happy?" WOW. With that question, they were asking for permission to really get to know me. And you know what? It felt good.

House of Cards

The Perfect Lie is like a slowly built house of cards. The deeper we fall into the Perfect Lie, the more we perceive others' opinions of our shortcomings as a threat to this house of cards. The Perfect Lie makes us worry more about the perceived truth rather than the actual truth.

Sometimes it can be hard to see how much this can undercut our ability to fully participate in a generous life. When we're living the Perfect Lie, it can be almost impossible to receive the generosity offered by someone. For example, I am sure we have all been on the receiving end of praise we didn't feel worthy of. At first, our feelings of unworthiness might persuade us to try to resist the compliment, but most of us—out of our sense of obligation—end up accepting it anyway.

The question is, what do we do with it? Most of us dismiss it and rationalize why the person gave it to us: "They were just trying to be nice," or "If they only knew the real story..." or "They just wanted to feel better about themselves."

No matter what reasoning we may invent, the fact remains that we never truly received the gift, and therefore we can't be grateful for it.

For me, sometimes it's hard to accept generosity. It's always easier to give than to accept. Because, subconsciously, receiving generosity compromises the narrative of the Perfect Lie. That is, it goes against that part of us that insists, "I don't need generosity." What we're really saying is, "You're offering to give me what I lack, and that threatens to destroy the carefully crafted story I have told—that I lack nothing or at least nothing important." The Perfect Lie obscures the way we see others and the way we think others perceive us.

On the other hand, even though we are trying to be "perfect," inside, we know we really aren't. We feel like frauds. And therefore, we don't feel worthy of generosity. We've told ourselves, "I am not a worthy person, I'm not as good as they are." Yet, we want to be *perceived* as being "good people." Before long, something has to give, and the house of cards comes tumbling down.

Hidden Daggers

True generosity is a lot like shaking hands. The handshake gesture began in ancient Greece as a way of conveying peaceful intentions. By extending empty right hands, strangers could show that they were not holding weapons and bore no ill will toward one another.

The up and down motion of shaking hands was designed to prove that you didn't have any daggers or any other weapons up your sleeve—the shaking motion would shake out anything hidden. This signified that both parties were coming with good intentions, wanting to build a relationship of peace.

Metaphorically speaking, sometimes we may do a good job of extending our hands—going through the motion of clasping hands, anyway. But when it comes time for the shaking we tend to pull back. Instead of shaking up and down, we hold the handshake still, just clasping, or we pull out altogether. The natural tendency is to hold back from shaking if we have something hidden up our sleeves.?

In large part, those hidden weapons are our insecurities. When we feel insecure about something, in order to avoid personal responsibility, we blame other people, or we blame circumstances. Because of our insecurities, we back away entirely from the relationship. We justify and shift the blame to make ourselves feel better so we don't have to change. When we don't shake hands, or refuse to show our insecurities, we are not fully committed to the relationship. When that happens, generosity cannot flourish.

In *The Go-Giver*, Bob Burg and John David Mann discuss five laws of stratospheric success.[10] One of the laws is authenticity. It is for good reason too, because the greatest act of generosity is sharing who you are with others:

Debra Davenport (Fictional Character, 'The Go-Giver')

As long as you're trying to be someone else, or putting on some act or behaviour someone else taught you, you have no possibility of truly reaching people. The most valuable thing you have to give people is yourself. No matter what you think you're selling, what you are really offering is you.

Concealing our insecurities and vulnerabilities makes it impossible to ever truly be at peace with ourselves and those around us. Imagine a hand that is clutching insecurities so tightly that it's formed a fist. No matter how earnest your desire to shake another's outstretched hand, you're simply unable to shake. That's what it's like when we refuse to let go of our insecurities, refuse to let someone see what's inside that clenched fist. No matter how convincingly we go through the motions, we're not ready to receive connection and deep, meaningful relationships.

The Perfect Lie Cycle

When we see ourselves as unworthy, it is hard to see others as worthy.

John Joseph Powell, a Jesuit priest and author said, "Why am I afraid to tell you WHO I AM? I am afraid to tell you WHO I AM, because if I tell you WHO I AM, you may not like WHO I AM, and it's ALL THAT I HAVE!"[11]

Insecurities come from the expectation we have of perfection. As humans, we were all designed to be imperfect. This is the beauty of it—none of us escape this fate, no matter how carefully and eloquently we sanitize the narrative of our lives. Life is one experiment after the other, and it would do the world well if we would share our results of what works or doesn't with each other.

On the occasion we empty our hand and extend it for a handshake as a show of peace, all too often the relationship crumbles because of the insecurities we have stowed away in our sleeve. These insecurities shake loose with the tumult of life. When those insecurities rear their ugly heads, they corrode and undermine our relationships.

When we approach generosity honestly—acknowledging our own insecurities while understanding that everyone falls short in some way—it allows us to be the receiver of generosity as much as it prompts us to be the giver of it. When we see others like we see ourselves, we can start to comprehend our need for each other. We can start to see the value in others' circumstances and struggles.

The Generosity Experiment made me aware of the insecurities I was holding in my own outstretched hand. As long as I was unconsciously concerned about how being generous would reveal my own unworthiness, I would never be able to fully comprehend how worthy others were of generosity. We are wired to struggle and to make mistakes, but we are all worthy of love and belonging.

Essentially The Perfect Lie Cycle can be broken down like this:

1. We see others as perfect, and therefore they are not like us. (They are perfect, we are not.)

2. We want to fit in, so we try to fit into the "perfect" mold we have in our minds. We hide our imperfections. We are not authentic.

3. We don't accept generosity because of the fear that it would reveal who we really are.

4. We don't give generosity because we won't show our insecurities or bond with others.

Without even realizing it, so many of us have fallen into this cycle, and it can be hard and even scary to think about bringing our insecurity and vulnerabilities out of the shadows, letting our authenticity shine.

Heart at War

If someone wants a deep, personal relationship with you, and you start to feel uncomfortable, it's because you are not ready to see *yourself* raw, unhidden by that careful narrative you created. They are allowing you to see what is inside of them. They are sharing their vulnerabilities, and you may panic because you don't want to reciprocate. You realize that what is inside of you scares you. Because it's a lie. You are trying to be perfect, but you aren't.

Fear of intimacy often affects our relationships. While there are times when we are aware of being hesitant and distrusting of generosity or friendship, we are more likely to identify these fears as concern over potentially negative outcomes: rejection, the deterioration of a relationship or feelings of affection that aren't returned.

Interestingly enough, our fear of connection is often triggered by positive emotions, even more so than negative ones. Experiencing love can often arouse deep-seated fears of intimacy and make it difficult to maintain a close relationship.

It might surprise you to know that real resistance to connection doesn't come from the acts of other people, but from an enemy within us. The problem is that the positive way someone sees us often conflicts with the negative ways we view ourselves. Sadly, we hold on to our negative attitude about ourselves and resist being seen differently. This is because it is difficult for us to allow the reality of being loved to affect our basic image of ourselves. We often build up a resistance to love.

A lot of these negative beliefs are based on feelings that we developed throughout our lives of being bad, unlovable or deficient. While these attitudes may be painful or unpleasant, at the same time they are familiar to us, and we are accustomed to them lingering in our subconscious. As adults, we mistakenly assume that these beliefs are fundamental to our being and therefore impossible to correct.

Our fear of rejection has strong roots in our insecurities. Our ability to be generous and see other people as worthy of generosity is directly impacted by our own set of insecurities, coupled with the self-image we hold of ourselves.

Here's the honest truth: None of us are perfect.

So enough already. We don't have to be "perfect"!

YOU DON'T HAVE TO BE PERFECT!!

Isn't that a relief?

Now we can let go and be authentic. When we don't have any hidden daggers. We are ready to connect with others and be genuine. Becoming more accepting of generosity and more willing to give generously.

When we see the TRUTH in others, we tend to see more that makes us the same. We are all imperfect! We all need generosity. We are all worthy of it. At one time or another we've all bought into the idea that *getting* is good, but *receiving* isn't good. WHY?

One of the more profound lessons I learned during my experiment was that there is no boundaries when it comes to generosity, I figured that it would mostly consist of my giving to "the needy." For me, that looked like donating money, food, and clothing to organizations that served "the poor." I had formed in my mind the type of person that needed generosity. But during the Experiment, I realized that I'm a horrible, horrible judge of who needs generosity and who doesn't.

The most important thing I learned is that generosity is *always good to offer to everyone*. Sure, you have to have your own compass and barometer and priorities of who and how you want to serve. Be true to that. For me, I wanted to honor my instincts; I wanted to act every time I felt a pull to help someone, even if they fell outside my preconceived notions of "in need."

The Positive Truth

By now, I think you've gotten the idea: the key to unraveling your life from the Perfect Lie is openness with each other. But you may be wondering, does this mean I am supposed to share everything? When I extend my hand, should I be bearing my entire soul? Not necessarily.

There is a boundary for what you share, and that boundary may change depending on where you are sharing (are you in a public place, or are you having an intimate, private conversation?). How do you know if you should share something?

My first step is always to interrogate my intentions. I ask myself, What is in my heart? If your objective is to build the perception that you are perfect or hide insecurities, then you are not being true to who you are and aren't acting out of generosity. Don't share. If you are going through a hard time, and your objective is to gain sympathy or attention, then maybe now is not the best time to share. Just hold off a bit.

But if you discover that your motivation to share was sprung from a desire to forge a connection, or to help someone else, then share. When you are ready, share what a situation has taught you. Share that you are grateful for something in spite of a challenge because of the challenge.

Whenever I feel shy about sharing something I know I should, I tell myself this: "My experiences are not just mine but everyone's. I have the responsibility to share things, once I've learned the lesson that may help other people as well."

Seeing Yourself, Seeing Others

You would think generosity would be easy. It feels good, right? But it's such a complex emotional interaction. Our brains do so many things to make us feel good and look good and be good and be happy. All of these ulterior belief systems and rationalities come in and have the ability to confuse us.

We can find a myriad of reasons we are here on this earth, but chief among them is to connect with other people. And the only way we can truly connect is if we see ourselves first as we truly are.

I really thought I had a pretty good idea of what I would experience when I started my Generosity Experiment, I thought it might be fun, and sure I would become a better version of the person I already was. I did NOT expect to learn things that would change my worldview so profoundly and cause me to think in an entirely different way.

Why does giving a server a 50 percent tip rather than a 15 percent tip take justification? It's usually just a few dollars. Why is it so hard? We have so many limitations and rules. I didn't realize I had a "guidebook" imprinted in my head of who I should be generous to and what it should look like.

How amazing would it be if we could see people for who they really are? You have to be responsible, but allow people in. Open yourself. Clasp that hand and shake.

Our life experiences, both negative and positive, all have the ability to empower us. Let's take a look at the rudimentary way that batteries produce power. If I asked you which part of the battery you didn't need you would probably respond, "You need all of it," and you would be right. A battery has a positive—or *cathode*—and a negative—or *anode*—charge and both are necessary to produce power. There are chemicals that exist within each side of the battery, and when they are mixed by completing the circuit, the outcome is what produces the power.

Our lives are not much different then these batteries. We will have positive and negative experiences in our lives, but the learning that comes from experiences is what truly matters. Our reaction, much like the reaction between the positive and negative charges in a battery, has the potential to make the experiences meaningful in way they couldn't have been alone. What we learn can turn our experiences into power.

If all we do is hold on to our experiences without learning the lessons they are meant to teach us, eventually all that negative energy, with nowhere to go, will corrode us from the inside out.

Corrosion often manifests itself in bitterness and stress. Being authentic is not just sharing everything that we have going on in our life, but taking time to reflect and learn from each experience as well.

Challenge the Norm

Living the Perfect Lie often confines us to living in the boxes that are assigned to us by our culture. It can reaffirm our insecurities and deter us from carrying out our purpose and fulfilling our calling in life.

In the nineteenth century, most Americans assumed that there was a natural order to society, which placed men and women in different spheres. The ideal woman was submissive; her job was to be a meek, obedient, loving wife who was for the most part subservient to the men around her.

Regardless, there were some women who were determined to do what they felt was right even if it flew in the face of the common practices of the day. One such woman was Clara Barton, a nurse during the American Civil War.

Clara Barton believed she was worthy of doing amazing things. In a time when rights for women were being challenged, she saw herself as worthy. She was the only woman recorded in history up to that point, to have ventured onto the battlefield to rescue fallen soldiers.

Jack Gibbs was a soldier in the Civil War. After suffering a wound from a battle, he must have thought, "I will never make it home, not in one piece anyway." He lay there shifting his body from one side to the other on the cold, rocky, war-torn ground, each movement causing more pain than relief. Understanding little about medical wounds, he still knew that if he was to survive he must lie still. But Gibbs' chance of survival was fading fast, and he was starting to lose hope.

As he lay on the ground with the battle raging about him, he felt a cool sensation rush over him and he lost consciousness. When Jack opened his eyes next, he saw that he was no longer on the battlefield; he could hear the shots of gunfire far off. He woke up to a woman standing over him. I'm sure that at first, he was astonished that a woman was standing over him, because women didn't come on the battlefield. But there she was, and she had hoisted him up on a wagon!

At the time, this wasn't a woman's job. But Clara Barton didn't care. Even though society told her that she wasn't worthy or "supposed" to do such things, she didn't allow that to define her actions. She believed that not only was she worthy, but that she had an obligation to stand and serve. She was generous and selfless in the face of being told that she wasn't supposed to be doing this. Her fearless mindset led her to do great things that have had a ripple effect across centuries—after the Civil War was over, Clara Barton went on to become the founder of the American Red Cross.

Barton's selfless actions are the epitome of the generosity that I strive to embody. She had a instinct to help, and she didn't let anyone stop her.

Let go of the Perfect Lie. Allow others in. Banish society's insistence that you have to appear perfect. Be authentic, so you can receive and offer generosity. You are worthy and can do amazing things.

Clara Barton felt compelled to help wounded soldiers on the battlefield. What do you feel compelled to do?

A Change in Perspective

Kevin Hines got up one day in September of 2000 and boarded a bus to the Golden Gate Bridge. In the 2006 documentary, *The Bridge*,[12] he describes his great mental and emotional pain as he sobbed into his hands on the way to the bridge. He stood there on the side of the bridge for about forty minutes as tourists, joggers, and bikers passed him by. A woman stopped to ask if he would take a picture of her on the iconic bridge. He thought, "A picture! I'm about to kill myself, what is wrong with you?" as he took the camera from her. He couldn't believe that she didn't see the obvious tears in his eyes and his distress. He took the picture, handed her the camera, and she was on her way.

He turned from the traffic to the bay and said to himself "FUCK IT"! Nobody cares," taking the woman's lack of acknowledgement as proof. He then hurled himself over the bridge.

When his hands left the rail, Kevin was suddenly jolted out of the lie that his life was not worth living. He said that the second his body was falling through the air, he felt regret. The lies that had been running through his mind stopped, and his perspective changed. In the four second 75 mph fall to the water below, he thought, "No one is going to know I didn't want to die."

His mind had told him that no one loved him and that no one would care. That is how powerful our brains are. The expectation that life should be perfect leaves us in despair when we realize our lives won't be perfect and that they can even be hard at times.

Suicide is a result of the ultimate lie we tell ourselves: We aren't worthy of life. Whether it is because of mental illness, addiction, or a moment of despair, it makes no difference. Every life is worth living. Telling ourselves that no one could understand excuses us from sharing what is in our heart and mind; it is what leads people to a place of hopelessness. Most of us have the opportunity to change our perspective under less tragic circumstances than Kevin, so let's not pass any opportunity to open up.

There have been over 2,000 suicide attempts off the Golden Gate Bridge since it was built in 1937. Kevin is part of the 1% that survived the fall to the water. After floating back up to the top, a seal swam over to him and began circling him. The coast guard that rescued him from the water said that the current created by the seal circling him was the only thing keeping Kevin's head out of the water and keeping him from drowning.

Kevin said in his interview that although he thought at the time that no one cared, he now realizes that he has a large network of people that care very much. Now he shares his vulnerable story for the whole world to hear. He is leveraging his experience to help others who may be victims of the same lie that nearly cost him his life. I often wonder whether I would have pushed myself out of my comfort zone to have a 10 percent moment and start a conversation with Kevin that day on the bridge. One thing I know for sure is that I am a lot more likely to have that conversation the more I practice.

Chapter 6 Challenges:

- *List all the insecurities that you can think of that could prevent you from receiving and giving generosity. Explain how these insecurities are probably part of the Perfect Lie.*

- *Check your sleeves for hidden daggers. Which insecurities keep you from creating deep, meaningful connections with others?*

- *Become the person you want to be. Write down a description of who he or she is.*

Chapter 7
Intention

You must be the change you wish to see in the world. —Mahatma Gandhi

The old adage "good things come to those who wait" might work with things like building a savings account—but it doesn't work with generosity. If you *wait* for a generous spirit to strike you, you will find yourself constantly sitting on the sidelines, missing opportunities.

I had gone my whole life thinking I was a pretty generous person, and, in fact, according to popular culture, I was a generous person. I did what was expected of me day-to-day : I spent some Saturdays doing service projects, I would help someone move when they asked, I held doors for people, and I even donated to the occasional charity fundraiser. These actions were the growing body of evidence that I used to prove that I was a generous person.

As many of us do, I was moving through life with blinders on, telling myself I was not just doing "enough" to check generosity off my list of to-dos, but I was doing more than enough.

Many of you may be like I was, just going through the motions of generosity. Here's what I learned. It's not that we need to dedicate more time or money to being generous, it's that our lack of intention cause us to leave so much on the table.

As long as I didn't see what I had become conditioned to ignore, there was no way I could learn from these experiences.

One of the most effective adjustments I made during my Generosity Experiment was how I started each day: *with intention.*

Setting my intentions every morning to find someone who I could be generous to, took me from the passenger seat to right behind the wheel. I became the author of my story, deciding the role I would play. This not only made me aware of my own humanity, revealing to me how much each of us has in common with each other, but it made it possible for me to actually see others as people rather than as objects to be used, avoided, or overcome.

Setting a generous intention each day took me from living passively, accepting that whatever happened to be in my path was enough, to actually enjoying the path. AND it opened my eyes to new opportunities that I may not have even noticed or had the pleasure of exploring before.

> *"Every day, think as you wake up: Today I am fortunate to have woken up. I am alive, I have a precious human life. I am not going to waste it."* —The Dalai Lama

From the very beginning of my experiment, I started seeing countless opportunities each day to be generous. These were unexpected things that didn't take more time or money; it just took me being intentional to see it. Often, I would have experiences that I normally would have passed right by, but because I had set for myself an intention to be generous, I found myself in constant evaluation mode, seeing opportunities to give all around me all the time.

Caught in the Tide

Setting intention is not a "set and forget" technique. Intention requires action and preparation to be successful. You have to follow through. If you plan to take a fishing trip and you intend to catch fish, then you better take a fishing pole and bait.

Setting intentions without preparing is no different than wishing or hoping.

Just imagine if you were a member of an army that went to battle, unprepared, but fully intending, hoping, to win. Wouldn't that be unwise? It is no different for you and your plans for your life.

It is easy to be intentional for the big things, like what profession to go into or whether you should study for a test. Somehow when things don't appear to be as impactful, or when the opportunity occurs more frequently, we take them for granted and they become background noise. We weren't intentional about those "minor" choices, so we aren't prepared to reach for them. Then it's easier to say no.

There have been too many times in my life when I wished I could help in a given situation, but because I was not prepared, I couldn't step up. Not because I didn't have the means, but simply because I had not set an intention and followed up with preparation.

Now, I set an intention every morning to give throughout the day whenever I feel the need to do so. For instance, I try to always have small bills on me to give. I always try to leave on time or early for engagements because someone who is always running late rarely has time to stop and help.

There are countless things you can do to ensure you will carry out your intentions. Just ask yourself, what do I need to have in my "toolbox" to follow through with my intentions? There are ways common to all of us that we can be generous with others, like giving of our time and money . But if you pay close attention, you will find there are ways to be generous that are unique to you. These opportunities, I have found, are some of the most profound opportunities and provide the most impactful learning experiences. For example, perhaps you have the gift of listening, or find yourself with more free time to volunteer or stop to help others than most people do, or perhaps you are able to encourage the down-and-out like no one else can. When we engage our personal gifts in the service of others in the form generosity, we learn more about ourselves and our purpose, and, perhaps most importantly, we learn that we belong to something bigger than us.

It is like when you are putting together a puzzle, and you find a piece that you know goes in a specific place, but it won't fit until you have attached it to the pieces around it. You turn it one way and then another, looking at the shapes and colors of the other pieces, until you find the combination that makes it fit into its correct spot. As you sit back and admire the puzzle, you can't believe it was so hard to figure out because all put together it makes so much sense.

It is in those moments that we can begin to realize there is something more to learn. These moments show us that we "fit" into a bigger puzzle.

The ancient sages of India observed thousands of years ago that our destiny is ultimately shaped by our deepest intentions and desires. The classic Vedic text known as the *Upanishads* declares,

"You are what your deepest desire is. As your desire is, so is your intention. As your intention is, so is your will. As your will is, so is your deed. As your deed is, so is your destiny."[13]

Similarly, in Stephen R. Covey's book *7 Habits of Highly Effective People,* he wrote, "There is a mental (first) creation, and a physical (second) creation. The physical creation follows the mental, just as a building follows a blueprint. If you don't make a conscious effort to visualize who you are to be and what you want in life, then you empower other people and circumstances to shape you and your life by default."[14]

In addition to making literal plans to follow through with our intentions, we must mentally prepare to be generous before we can actually be generous with our actions. But this "first creation" is where so many of us fall short, so we end up having to take whatever scraps are left because our vision is impaired by our habits and the ease of the way.

Generosity is a tool that requires a "first" creation, or a spiritual vision. Each day can be better, no matter how good they are now, by being intentional about looking for every opportunity to be generous.

As a teenager, I went on a vacation to Hawaii with my family. I can remember each of us four kids were given twenty dollars for spending money. My brother and I were wandering around the hotel where we were staying and ended up at the excursion desk. The sign said *Snorkel Gear $7*. It had beautiful pictures of the reef and all the different types of fish you might see. The adventure also came with a roll of fish food to boot.

After doing the calculations to make sure that if we purchased this experience we would still have enough to buy a souvenir monkey made out of a coconut, we made the purchase. We thought it would be an amazing way to experience Hawaii.

The next day, early in the morning, we showed up to the desk to rent the gear. The staff member asked us if we had snorkeled in this reef before and if we wanted a quick lesson about where to go and what to look for. We were both good swimmers and had been snorkeling before, so we thought, "How different could this reef be from the others we had seen?" Needless to say, we declined his offer and took off to the reef on our own.

As typical teenagers, we had no thought of danger as we approached the ocean. After we got the goofing off and throwing fish food at each other out of the way, we put our heads down in the water. Immediately, we were immersed in the beauty of the underwater world. The plants and fish were vibrant and unlike anything I had ever seen before. I thought we had hit the jackpot. We were out there for quite a while, feeding the fish and soaking it all in.

After what felt like the whole morning, we finally popped our heads up out of the water and got our bearings. Because we hadn't had any real plan for how or where we were going to be snorkeling, we had no idea where we had ended up. We realized that we had actually drifted away from shore about three-fourths of a mile. We could still see the shore, but we were very far from it.

We were surprised and a little scared.

We started heading back to the shore, but what we didn't know was that we had been caught up in a current that flowed away from the beach. Had we taken the five minute lesson we were offered at the excursion desk, we might have avoided it. Getting back to shore was going to be a lot harder now.

But it was not so much the current that had put us in danger—after all, that current had always been there; it was our lack of planning and preparation that put us in harm's way.

It took everything we had to swim back to shore that day

Drifting is something that happens in life when we let the current take us, rather than making an intentional choice about where we want to go, how much risk we want to take, and what we want the result to be. When we are not intentional in our thoughts and actions, we allow the ebb and flow of life to dictate where we end up, rather than choosing the path that only we can know will make us happy.

The path I took under that Hawaii water was not an unattractive route! I was having fun, and it was exciting. I didn't realize, however, that I was putting myself in danger. We think the road to dangerous places is ugly or obviously *wrong*. That is not always the case. This reef was beautiful! It was simply unintentional, which ultimately ended up making it dangerous for me. If I had prepared and paid attention, keeping my eyes on where I intended to go, I would still have experienced the same beauty but avoided the unnecessary risk.

My experience underwater was so much like how we experience generosity. We allow ourselves to drift into these places where we are enjoying the ride; we are generous when the opportunity bumps into us because it is in the same current we happen to be in. Unless we are intentional about who we want to be and how we want to see others, it will be decided for us.

It is not that you set out to destroy your health, damage your most important relationships, or screw up a career, but it is the lack of a plan or vision which usually results in those decisions. Very few have ever drifted to a destination that they would have chosen if they had been conscious of it when they were doing the choosing.

Begin With the End in Mind

If you wait, nothing will happen.

When you are intentional about your desire to be generous, and prepare accordingly, you are ready for each opportunity. Certainly, having good experiences is possible even if we are drifting through life, but when we let drifting be our primary mode of transportation, we miss opportunities that may have transformative effects on our lives. Whether it is a connection, a lesson, or an understanding, missing it can leave us far away from the person we desire to be. In my literal drifting experience in the Pacific ocean, it required a lot more work to get back to safety, and I didn't enjoy the beauty that was beneath me anymore because I was so worried about being swallowed up by the sea.

I didn't have the end in mind when I went snorkeling. I should have started by taking the expert's advice and directions! I could have mapped out where to go. I needed to be intentional about my end goals—to *enjoy the beauty* and to *be safe*.

With generosity, it's the same thing. If I'm intentional about being generous, I see more opportunity. I get to act and feel in the moment.

When our intentions give us the ability to take an opportunity to be generous, we feel a sense of purpose and shared connection that we wouldn't get otherwise. In addition, we become proactive about enjoying experiences rather than just letting the experience wash over us.

I wanted to learn the most I could about generosity for my experiment, so I prepared. I dove into TED talks, YouTube videos, books, finding what others were doing to be generous. Through this, I figured out what to set my intention toward. That is, I understood what I wanted to get out of the experience—what my end goal was.

There are all types of generosity opportunities out there, and if you set your intention you *will* find them something.

By reading this book, you've taken the first step toward intentionality: you are asking for directions. You are considering the end, at the beginning. You are being intentional about figuring out how to prepare yourself for life of generosity. Are you committed to starting your own Generosity Experiment? As you read, start planning, so that when you close this book, you know exactly where to go next.

So many people fall short of achieving what they plan to because they are impaired by habit or they jump in without proper preparation. We do it all the time! For instance, have you ever bought something you had to put together yourself? Answer honestly: did you read the directions, or did you just try to figure it out as you went? I bet some of you even skipped the introduction of this book and jumped right into the first chapter.

If we believe we are the stewards of our lives, then we have to take control. The most powerful tool we have is our ability to choose. Are we letting habit and circumstance be in control, or are we being intentional in how we choose to live?

If you read Chapter 2, you may be wondering, "Now Jayson, if I'm supposed to be grateful for everything—including bad experiences—then why do my choices and intentions matter that much?"

No doubt about it, in retrospect, I was grateful for the learning opportunity of getting caught up in the current in Hawaii. But I don't want to do something like that again. It taught me something—*always* prepare, and if because of that experience, I'm intentional next time, I've benefitted from it.

Being intentional is the shortest pathway to getting out of your habit zone (the 90 percent) and into your

10 percent. As we learn through our experiences and set our intentions accordingly, we can grab the 10 percent outside of our comfort zone where the miracles happen. Those miracles can really help us connect and grow with others.

So, we have it now—be intentional and prepare—right? Yes, but here's one small admonition, because life is unpredictable: Set your intentions to be generous, but don't require a certain outcome. You can't control what others do or say. They could react to your offerings of generosity with gratitude, or they may react differently.

Have you ever started a fitness and nutrition regimen with a certain goal in mind—for example, to lose weight? How long does it take for you to jump on the scale to see how many pounds you have shed? You might be up a pound from drinking too much water or down two pounds because you stopped retaining water from all the soda you no longer consume.

Does the scale get in the way of being able to appreciate the process, being grateful for what your body is capable of? The constant measuring of body weight, the singular drive to reach your goal, can fast become obsession. Some things are out of your control. Don't be so attached to the outcome of your Generosity that you miss the magic that happens right in the middle of it.

Do you remember science lab in high school? We learned about all the different chemical reactions, or laws of physics, or observed natural patterns. And when we went to do our own minor experiments, sometimes we got the outcome we hypothesized we would get, and sometimes we didn't. But whatever the result, those experiments were never considered "failures", it was all a part of the process. We learned valuable things each time.

I like to think of life as a string of science experiments. We are going to have failures, sometime we're going to get an outcome we didn't expect. But know that just because something didn't work out like you thought, it doesn't mean it's a failure.

We tend to define ourselves by our insecurities. If we are generous to someone, and they don't accept our offering, it's like they aren't accepting us. And if they don't accept it/us, then we've failed.

It doesn't matter so much what the act or outcome itself is, *giving* is the success! Perhaps one of the greatest things to come out of a Generosity Experiment is not how people will thank you or who will be grateful for your kind acts. Perhaps the greatest of all the blessings you can receive is that generosity is a *way of being*. True generosity is not something you do, but it is consistently honoring others by loving them and seeing them as worthy.

One of my favorite books is *The Greatest Salesman in the World* by Og Mandino. In that book there is a poor camel boy, Hafid, who is able to achieve abundance and great success by applying what he finds on hidden scrolls. One of the scrolls is entitled, "Today I will greet this day with love in my heart."

The boy comes across this declaration:

"And how will I confront each whom I meet? In only one way. In silence and to myself I will address him and say I Love You. Though spoken in silence these words will shine in my eyes, unwrinkle my brow, bring a smile to my lips, and echo in my voice; and his heart will be opened. And who is there who will say nay to my goods when his hearts feels my love?"[15]

Hafid is discovering what it takes to not only be a success in sales, but to succeed in most aspects of life. Making this declaration and setting this intention for all encounters with others is the secret to living a full and abundant life.

As you start your own Generosity Experiment, set your intentions, notice opportunities as they come, and then act. Try it out. See what happens. The great thing is, every day you get to reset. You wake up and decide whether you're happy, whether you're going to honor your decision to live generously. YOU choose. You are the one in the driver's seat.

Slow and Steady: Choosing Your Path

Many times, when something isn't hurting us in the moment, we don't change. I was lucky in Hawaii—I could have been in real trouble. If I would have drifted too far, it would have been too late. Sometimes we wait until the consequences are immediate and real. If we aren't in pain right then, we don't change.

But, trust me when I say, your life will deteriorate slowly as you neglect the part of you that desires to be generous. After a few years, you look up and realize what could have been, but you are living beneath your potential because you weren't intentional.

How can generosity become more important in your daily life? It's not a To-Do List item. It's not checking something off. It's about developing a generous disposition. It's about seeing people the way you see yourself.

It's not about having time or money. You will find yourself making room for generosity in your life when you start seeing people the way we were intended to see each other. Generosity is a muscle you have to develop over time. I hope this book will be a crash course in helping you see people in their humanity, as someone just like you.

Have you ever completed one of those questionnaires that is supposed to determine your future career? The thing is, we often know what we want to be, so we can skew our answers to fit what we want the outcome to be. We want an answer immediately, without doing the slow and steady work.

What we are going to be happiest doing is tailor-made for us. Most often, it is not made known to us until we have taken action, and it usually requires not just one or two actions, but consistently setting your intention to honor what you feel. Finding what fulfills us will usually reveal itself after living in service of others.

At one juncture in my life, I set criteria of what I thought would fulfill me, in terms of a career. I wanted to make enough money, have free time, work the way I wanted to, etc. I made a list of what I believed was important. When I had settled on a career I thought would meet the criteria, I took the necessary licensing tests, and I became a certified insurance agent. I thought this was the answer, it had to be! It met all the criteria I had set.

A month into my new job, I realized it was not going to work! I quit. Then, I changed the way I thought about life. I chose to meet my destiny rather than force it. As I started working on myself and honoring the opportunities that came my way and the promptings I felt, my Generosity Experiment, public speaking, and this book started coming together.

All along the way, I could feel my life speaking to me, telling me that this is what was right! To think, I had set the terms for what this life had to offer me. It was like I had cheated on the career placement test to manufacture the outcome I wanted. I was not BECOMING someone. This other, better path that ultimately unfolded is helping me become a better person, the person I need to be.

When we honor the sense we have to do something, then we *become*. It is hard, and a lot of the time it is scary. But if we focus more on the process then we do on the outcome, we can find security in knowing we are on the right path.

Generosity helps you become authentic and true to who you are. Get out of the box of expectation you have been assigned by society. Once you get out, it will feel amazing. You will feel a sense of relief. It's really a form of compassion and generosity to yourself.

What is the one thing I could achieve today to make it great?

When you stop to ask this question, you instinctively scan your internal To-Do List and weed out things that (turns out!) don't matter and focus instead on the one or two things that will truly bring some measure of happiness.

By creating an intention, we suddenly know how to measure our day. We connect with the goal behind the goal. I don't think any of us just want to "work." We *actually* want to achieve a feeling of security, a sense of purpose, or a monetary reward. Or all three.

Connecting with your ultimate goal, the end you have in mind or the person you want to become, helps you to bypass everything else and focuses your power in a way that makes your days more meaningful. If we don't stop to ponder what we want to achieve, then our days—our lives!—just slip away.

It's within your ability to harness this power, but it's up to you to put into practice.

5 Practical Steps to Generosity

1. **Decide to live *your* life.** Stop comparing yourself to others. You were not born to live their life. There is no sense wasting yours

being jealous of theirs. Instead, you were born to live your life–determine today to be good at it. After all, you only get one shot.

2. **Define a purpose.** Identify what you want your life to communicate to others and contribute to the world. Find a passion to live for, something bigger than yourself. Write it down. It will bring new meaning to your life. It will wake you from the slow death of only living for yourself.

3. **Set goals.** Goals move us and goals shape us. Set goals that are directly in line with your defined purpose. By their very nature, they will introduce intentionality into your life.

4. **Stay focused.** We live in a world of constant connectivity and distraction that is begging for our attention nearly every moment of the day. Learn to turn off the distractions and live your life instead.* Turn off the TV and don't read gossip magazines. Remove nonessential physical belongings that are robbing you of time and energy that could be better spent living intentionally.

   Example: Take the Phone Challenge. (See Chapter 7 Challenges: page 152) .

5. **Learn from others.** Successful people are curious people. They possess the humility to learn from others. Identify people accomplishing a purpose similar to yours. Then, study them and learn from them.

Chapter 7 Challenges:

- *Start setting your generous intentions for each day. Write them down!*

- *Could you benefit from a deliberate effort to stay more focused? Try the* **Take the Phone Challenge:**

    1- No phone at the dinner table.

    2- No charging the phone in your bedroom at night (the first and last iteration of the day should not be with a phone).

    3- No phone in the waiting room. (Set a goal to have at least one conversation as you wait.)

    4- Take it out of your pocket at home (be present).

- *Identify the areas in your day to day life where you are missing out on the chance to participate in generosity and make an intentional choice to be prepared to engage when you next opportunity comes.*

Chapter 8
Generosity is in Our DNA

"It was easy to love God in all that was beautiful. The Lessons of deeper Knowledge, though, instructed me to embrace God in all things." —St. Francis Of Assisi

Our Strongest Instinct

In 1871, eleven years before his death, Charles Darwin published what has been called his greatest unread book: *The Descent of Man and Selection in Relation to Sex*. His discussion of sympathy in this book is in steep contrast to the competitive, ruthless, and selfish view of human nature that has been so widely attributed to most of Darwin's work.

In the fourth chapter, entitled "Comparison of the Mental Powers of Man and the Lower Animals," Darwin discusses the origin of what he calls *sympathy*, (but what we would term today as *empathy*) describing how humans and animals come to the aid of others in distress. Here he tells the following story:[16]

> Several years ago a keeper at the Zoological Gardens showed me some deep and scarcely healed wounds on the nape of his own neck, inflicted on him whilst kneeling on the floor, by a fierce baboon. The little American monkey who was a warm friend of this keeper, lived in the same compartment, and was dreadfully afraid of the great baboon. Nevertheless, as soon as he saw his friend in peril, he rushed to the rescue, and by screams and bites so distracted the baboon that the man was able to escape.

Darwin also notes that exceptional people will help total strangers in distress, not just kin or loved ones.

> Nevertheless many a civilized man who never before risked his life for another, but full of courage and sympathy, has disregarded the instinct of self-preservation and plunged at once into a torrent to save a drowning man, though a stranger. In this case man is impelled by the same instinctive motive, which made the heroic little American monkey, formerly described, save his keeper by attacking the great and dreadful baboon.[17]

Darwin concludes by defining what he considered the "highest moral virtue":

> As man advances in civilization, and small tribes are united into larger communities,

> the simplest reason would tell each individual that he ought to extend his social instincts and sympathies to all members of the same nation, though personally unknown to him. This point being once reached, there is only an artificial barrier to prevent his sympathies extending to the men of all nations and races.

So, was Darwin right? Are *sympathy, empathy, generosity* humanity's highest moral virtues? Our greatest achievements? Our strongest instincts? Well, let's think about how we have evolved as a species. Despite millions of years of natural selection, we are not fast, we are not strong, we have not grown fangs, we don't have the muscle mass primates do. Because perhaps that isn't why we're here—it's something else entirely that has led to the perpetuation of our species. What humans have is the ability to cooperate and take care of others.

The ideas Darwin laid out in *The Descent* are evident in the world all around us. Not only do we have the unique ability to cooperate with each other, we have a primal *need* to get along. Humanity's evolution is less about muscle mass and keen physical ability and more about community and cooperation. Love is not only what brings people into the world, it is the fuel for our survival.

There is however, a contrasting view: some believe the goal human interaction to be domination, not cooperation. You don't have to look very far to find examples of how domination has gone wrong. A unit as small as a family with a dominating parent or an entity as large as a country with a dictator, both usually end up in disarray because the children, or the nation's people feel displaced. As we combine our experiences and cooperate to pursue the collective good, we see others as partners rather than adversaries. In that light, we stand to achieve far more.

It's Biology

By our very nature, we crave connection. That is, we are biologically designed to connect. One example of this is the chemical oxytocin.

Oxytocin is known colloquially as the "love hormone." Its influence on our behavior and physiology originates in the brain, or more specifically, the hypothalamus. From there, it's transferred to the pituitary gland, which releases it into the bloodstream. Like antennas picking up a signal, oxytocin receptors, found on cells throughout the body, sense when the chemical is flooding through the blood.

According to Carol Rinkleib Ellison, a clinical psychologist in Loomis, California, and former assistant clinical psychiatry professor at the University of California, San Francisco, it's this "love hormone" that creates feelings of calm and, importantly, the sense of closeness to other people.

There have been numerous studies conducted on how oxytocin affects social interaction, and the results are clear: this chemical is a boon for sympathy, empathy, and generosity.

For example, a study in *Proceedings of the National Academy of Sciences* showed that inhaling synthetic oxytocin significantly improved the ability of people with autism to interact with others, effectively promoting social interaction and connection.

In a 2007 study in *Public Library of Science ONE*[18], participants inhaled either oxytocin or a placebo through their noses, and then were asked to decide how to split money with a stranger. Results showed that those who had inhaled oxytocin were eighty percent more generous.

A study performed by the Claremont Graduate University School of Organizational and Behavioral Studies and Center for Neuroeconomics Studies found that empathy was associated with a forty-seven percent increase in oxytocin. The study also found that higher levels of empathy were also associated with more generous monetary offers toward strangers. The findings provide evidence that oxytocin is a physiologic signature for empathy and, moreover, that empathy mediates generosity.

Have I lost anyone yet? This chapter was not designed to be a biology class, but I did want to make it clear that we were designed to connect with each other. We are acting most in line with our nature when we practice empathy and generosity.

I've often heard people say something along the lines of, "the highest form of giving is to expect nothing in return." I think what they mean is that giving without expecting an equal reciprocation feels the best, the most moral. True altruism is considered "high giving." But I'd argue that the most selfless givers *do* receive something in return: a richer and more abundant life (and a host of good feelings, thanks to oxytocin).

That Strange Phenomenon Empathy

In Chapter Seven, we talked about being intentionally generous. Even though we produce a natural chemical that helps us bond it doesn't happen spontaneously. You can't bond with a stranger just by being in the same room together. You must *actively seek the other person*. Making the choice is what ignites bonding.

While you forge strong bonds with your family and friends through constant and consistent connecting, you can bond with others even through just a few isolated instances and still have an impact on their lives and your own happiness.

Psychologist Abigail Marsh shares a story in her TED Talk about altruism.[19] She was headed home to Tacoma, Washington, on a school break. She was on the interstate and a dog happened to run out in front of her car. She made the mistake of swerving to avoid it and then over-correcting, which ended with her hitting a side rail and stalling broadside in the middle of the fast lane.

The next thing she remembered was a knock on the window and a man telling her she looked like she needed help. He got in, pushed her into the passenger seat, sped across the freeway, and parked safely on the side of the road. After making sure she was okay and didn't need any more help, he let the paramedics take over and he left. Never to see her again.

In reflection of this moment, it baffled Abbey as to why a complete stranger would risk his life to help her, with no expectation of any kind of claim or payoff.

In these moments, it is easy to think that the only person who benefitted from the interaction was Abbey. And while it may seem strange, this man is not alone in his act of extreme generosity—stories like Abbey's are, if not commonplace, certainly not rare. Anytime we honor the natural impulse of generosity, we gain something important, a set of tangible skills and beliefs that make us better at being human.

Our confidence about who we are and our role among everyone around us is possibly the most significant outcome of these types of moments. When we embrace empathy, it requires us to see others as we see ourselves, and in turn, changes the way we see the world.

In a Q&A, Amy Banks, M.D., author of *Relationships and Brain Chemistry*, was asked what happens when people are not connected with others.[20]

She replied,

> I believe one of the seminal studies that supports a relational neurobiology is something called SPOT (Social Pain Overlap Theory). This theory is best described in a study conducted by UCLA researchers. They

looked at the overlap between social pain and physical pain. They designed a benign computerized experiment that gradually excluded people from a multi-player game. What they found was the area that lit up in the brain for that kind of social rejection—the anterior cingulate—was the exact same area that lights up for the distress of physical pain.

So, the distress of social pain is biologically identical to the distress of physical pain. Most people in our culture understand that physical pain is a major stressor, but we often reject the idea of social pain. This impacts our society on a grand scale, for example look at instances of racism or homophobia—any of the ways that we stratify and divide our social structures can literally cause pain.

Noted neurobiologist Jonathan Haight said that when he asked people their reasons for helping someone in trouble, they all gave the same basic response: a drive to help because it made them feel good, a sensation which Haight later came to call *elevation*.[21]

So now we understand how acting on our empathy benefits us, but what causes us to be able to empathize in the first place?

The discovery of mirror neurons is fast becoming one of the most talked about things in behavioral science. Mirror neurons are found in the frontal lobes of the brain, embedded among motor command neurons. Motor neurons fire when you reach out to grab something, when you push something, when you hit something, etc. They orchestrate a sequence of muscle twitches to allow you to make significant movements.

But there's a subset of motor neurons that fire when you simply watch another person, these are called mirror neurons. When I watch someone else reach out and grab something, my mirror neurons react as if I was the one making the action.

Mirror neurons have given us insight as to why people are generous, sometimes even to their own detriment, in situations where they have the opportunity to help a complete stranger. Mirror neurons enable us to see others as intentional beings, just like us.

What we think and feel affects others. Have you ever walked into a room where two people have just been in a heated argument? Despite any efforts to disguise the discontent in the room, you still feel the tension.

Albert Einstein called this the "spooky action at a distance." Scientists conducted tests with neurons. They gathered people in a room and monitored the action of the neurons; over time, the neurons of different people were able to communicate or connect in some unknowable way. They would mimic the movement of the neurons of the other people in the study.

It is this theory that helps us explain why we can feel the energy of a room and that of another person.

The way we see others, the way we feel, and the way we think has an effect on the people around us whether we speak it out loud or not.

Developing Empathy Through Service

As someone who, by nature, likes to challenge the status quo, I have long rebelled against the pervasive idea, especially in western cultures, that women are more fit and capable than men when it comes to the rearing and nurturing of children.

I wanted to use the topic of parenting in this chapter because we hear so much in our culture that "some things just are the way they are." Men have lost in the contest of perceived potential for compassion or empathy, especially in regards to parenting—and there's a reason that goes beyond "things are the way they are."

The thing is, if fathers aren't the ones raising their kids, they won't have the levels of empathy for them as mothers do. Why? Not because they *naturally* aren't built for the job, but because *the key to empathy is service.*

Mothers have some distinct advantages in this area. The most obvious ones are the facts surrounding childbearing. Women utilize their bodies for nine months in complete service of the infant, so women already have a nine-month head start. And then even after the child is born, in Western culture, it is common for the women to be at home with the child, and the father may not even miss a day of work. (Now, if the father buys into the idea that raising children is the woman's job anyway, he may not be likely to run home after work to change diapers and make dinner in service of his children. Instead he might chalk up the day of hard work at the office as service enough and head to the bar for drinks with the guys.)

You love those for whom you serve. A mother's intuition doesn't just *happen* to new mothers; it is earned through service. Feeling close to those you serve is made possible because of the deepening effects that service has on your ability to empathize.

There was a time when I was the primary caregiver to our kids. I was a stay-at-home-dad. When I switched from spending time working outside the home to spending time serving my kids in the home, I came to understand that many of the beliefs I held as facts were a very fluid concept. There was a lot more to the story then the *"women are just better with kids"* narrative I had bought into..

I bandaged their scrapes, made their lunches, helped settle fights, noticed their likes and dislikes, helped them with their fears. I was in their direct service all day long. When you are constantly focusing on someone besides yourself, you become more aware of the love you have for them.

Not only is empathy fostered through service, but we perceive love through the service others do for us as well. Going to work to earn money is necessary to sustain life, and is service in its own way, but it isn't as intimate or personal as a hug or being there when your children need you. It doesn't produce the in-person connection that we crave.

Remember this as you develop your own Generosity Experiment. If you claim you aren't naturally "good at connecting with others", you are selling yourself short. Even if you don't have those skills right now, it doesn't mean you can't work to develop them—you can increase your empathy and your ability to bond with those around you through service.

If you're shy, it truly may be harder for you to learn to connect with others. But it's a skill you can grow int! An outgoing person may have an advantage with immediate connections because he or she is more open and talkative. But you, the naturally shy person, may have a natural ability to intuit what other people need.

> "Keep feeling the need to be first. But I want you to be first in Love. I want you to be first in moral excellence. I want you to be first in generosity." — Martin Luther King, Jr.

Connection is an active choice we make. One thing I realized during my experiment is that it wasn't necessarily personal relationships that helped me feel connected. I've been able to be generous and help people with just a smile or changing a tire on the side of the road for people I don't know.

Below I've included a few strategies to further increase your empathy:

1. Pay it Forward

The term "pay it forward" was popularized by Robert A. Heinlein in his book *Between Planets*, first published in 1951[22]:

> The banker reached into the folds of his gown, pulled out a single credit note. "But eat first—a full belly steadies the judgment. Do me the honor of accepting this as our welcome to the newcomer."
>
> His pride said no; his stomach said YES! Don took it and said, "Uh, thanks! That's awfully kind of you. I'll pay it back, first chance."
>
> "Instead, pay it forward to some other brother who needs it."

The idea that you help someone who will in turn help someone else in the future is a practice that allows us to play a positive role in our individual communities. It could be our family, neighborhood, business, or city, but any way you dice it, the more people being generous to each other the better.

Ralph Waldo Emerson, in his 1841 essay *Compensation*, wrote: "In the order of nature we cannot render benefits to those from whom we receive them, or only seldom. But the benefit we receive must be rendered again, line for line, deed for deed, cent for cent, to somebody."

There is no quid pro quo when generosity is at its best. We can take heart in knowing when we are an active participant in connecting with others. Paying it forward is the idea that the power to change the world resides in each of us.

Connecting through generosity generates worthiness in you and the other person.

In Brené Brown's research on shame, she found that the one the thing that keeps us out of connection is our fear that we are not worthy of connection: "The one variable that separated those who had a strong sense of love and belonging and those that struggled for it was that those who have the strong sense of love and belonging believe they are worthy of love and belonging."

While generosity and the desire to connect with other human beings are in our DNA, they are not in the fabric of our society. Resisting the powerful draw of what is culturally accepted and instead giving in to the natural inclination toward empathy will be one of the hardest things to embrace, at least at first.

2. Begin with Trust

Have you ever had a magician show you a magic trick that completely baffled you? Most of us have had an experience where we have been totally duped by a magician's clever tricks.

Why is this so common?

It is not because you are gullible, it is because your brain decided to trust what your eyes saw. Humans have been hardwired to trust since the beginning of time. Trust is the default setting for most of us.

Can you imagine a world without trust? A simple a task as driving down the road is all about trust; for people to be able to speed down a highway at seventy miles per hour with only a painted line separating them from oncoming traffic requires major trust—but we trust those other drivers (for the most part) without giving it a second thought.

We trust in all sorts of situations. It might be at the checkout in the grocery store when you are receiving change, or when you are told you need surgery and a doctor you have never met is going to be holding your life in his hands.

Trust is rewarded in our brain by the hypothalamus releasing that feel-good chemical—yup you guessed, it good old oxytocin. Our biology encourages us to trust because without trust we could not survive.

You must cultivate and develop trust over time. In a relationship with another person, trust is built with deposits and reciprocation. In society and our relationship with the population at large, it works a little differently. Trust becomes more about what you look for than what is reciprocated.

If I'm constantly focused on what I am grateful for, to whom I can be generous, and how others have been generous to me, then my trust level will rise. My ability to bond with, influence, and connect with others will also increase.

Being cynical and distrusting is not always a matter of looking for the opposite of what breeds trust. More often than not, people are not looking for the worst in others; but when we are not intentional about what we are looking for it easy to drift as I did with my snorkeling adventure in Hawaii.

"This is an extremely difficult command far from being the pious injunction of a utopian dreamer. This command is an absolute necessity for the survival of our civilization. Yes, it is love that will save our world and our civilization, love even for our enemies."

Martin Luther King, Jr., frequently found himself in situations where the easy road would have been to promote violence and vengeance; many would have believed him to be justified in doing so. He understood a deeper purpose for the plight of the black person of his time. He counseled the people who followed him to cultivate the things that increased love, gratitude, and connection, even in the face of violence.

One of the great insights of King was to tell his followers that the racist enemies persecuting you are damaged human beings. You have the power to liberate them from their own damaged souls. That by following the path of love you are giving them the opportunity to become fully human. They become no more the all-powerful oppressor.

In the end, you are making connections. You are showing love. The ultimate test, I believe, of a generous life is who you become.

Chapter 8 Challenge:

- *Identify a person or a group of people you may have preconceived notions about. Once you have identified them devise a plan to serve them.*

- *Take inventory of your life and ask yourself if there is anywhere that you are not promoting generous behaviour. List the rationalizations you are giving that makes it okay.*

- *You can take satisfaction to know that you belong to the human race. Take action to help someone they belong as well.*

Chapter 9
Before You Begin Your Experiment

*Guard your time fiercely. Be generous with it,
but be intentional about it.
—David Duchemin, humanitarian
photographer*

Over the years, there have been countless graduation speeches given by celebrities, CEO's or other successful people to inspire the graduates who are finishing their studies and going out into the world. No doubt these graduates are looking forward to launching their careers, starting families, and embarking on new adventures. They want to know: What is going to matter most?

You must help others.

This is the piece of advice that is most pertinent to the next generation of graduates. *Whatever you do, go out and make a difference and help others, giving is the secret to life, giving is the key to receiving*, we are told.

Hopefully those graduates will take that message to heart and that will translate into action, a way of life, and eventually, part of their who they are. Unfortunately, we all get comfortable in our routines and habits. Part of that routine inevitably includes some sort of generous acts, but it's all within our carefully crafted comfort zones. How can we actually change?

In a way, you are like that graduate. You are opening a new chapter—no matter where in life you happen to be right now. Starting today, you can begin a grand new adventure. For eight chapters, you've been reading about my Generosity Experiment. Are you ready to change? Are you ready to start your *own* Generosity Experiment?

Before you jump in, a few things to consider.

Avoid Burnout

Most people know Richard Simmons as the very energetic exercise guru with short shorts and a big smile. But he was more than that. He truly cared about and wanted to help people. There was a specific type of person he was drawn to—those who wanted to connect personally.

While many people simply bought his workout videos and never interacted with him, there were others who sought him out in person, and he responded.

He wanted to touch others. Simmons turned himself inside out trying to give everyone of his followers whatever they wanted.

Simmons was a giving person, but he gave to the point of burnout. So for a long time, he left the limelight. The short story was that his energy was spent and because of that, connecting the way he had been used to, had become a lot harder. By giving and giving and giving, he had given until he had nothing left. Eventually he didn't have the ability to give at the level he had been accustomed to anymore. It was unsustainable giving.

When we give everything we have, we burn ourselves out. So, how do you avoid burnout but still be generous?

Linda Holmes, of National Public Radio, offered a poignant explanation of what can happen when we give to the extreme without even realizing it.

> I have pinned to my cubicle walls almost every paper note and letter I've ever received from readers and listeners. But, speaking metaphorically, not every expression of gratitude arrives on paper, which you can keep with you, pinned to your life indefinitely. Some thank-you's arrive written on rocks, and if you feel obligated to carry all of those rocks everywhere you go for the rest of your life, if you can't learn to look at them, be grateful for them, and set them down, even they become a lot to carry.

> The more the gratitude is for what has already been done, the more it is written on paper: *I'm so grateful for the thing you made; it meant the world to me.* That is weightless; it is wonderful. The closer it gets to expecting something from you in the future, something that must continue, the more it is written on stone: *You're the only one who understands me. You're the only reason I can get out of bed every day.*[23]

I have a feeling that Simmons received a lot of gratitude written on stones, just as many generous people do. For Simmons, those stones were hard to put down.

Even though most of us could definitely give more, we are all in jeopardy of burnout. Ask yourself this question: Are you giving out of obligation, to fill the generosity quota that the world has placed on you. Are you giving to feel needed and special?

Or are you generous because you see others as simply being worthy of it? Are you being generous as a pathway to connect with others?

As you identify your generous motivations you will be able to map out a clear course having the freedom to become the person you desire to be.

Generosity should be weightless. It should be freeing.

Be Wary of Takers

Sometimes you'll encounter people who clutch at those who give freely; they are thankful, but they also want to be given more and more. These people are the

Takers. They are seeking someone who will give and give, and they will take and take in equal measure. They'll hand stones to you which read, "I don't know how I will get along without you."

As you are learning how to better identify takers you can be satisfied that you were generous to them. But it's important to draw a line in the sand. Just because someone continues to ask does not mean you have to continue to give. In fact, sometimes it is not a matter of giving them what they want, rather it becomes about giving them what they need.

Sometimes telling someone no is the most generous thing you can do for them. Don't give more than you have. If you do that, you'll quickly find, that as you lug around those "gratitude" stones, they will start to overwhelm you and your legs will begin to buckle under the weight. Even small stones carried for long periods of time can create stress and discomfort.

The most emotionally healthy people I've met are capable of extending generosity to others, while at the same time putting a line in the sand. They know when to say no. For example, I wouldn't ask a mere acquaintance to babysit my kids, and they wouldn't ask to crash on my couch. It's not apathy or superiority or disdain. There is only so much energy that each of us has. When energy runs low, it runs out. And then where are you? If you're exhausted, you are unable to be generous at all.

Recognize the requests of Takers, then set them down. Don't be attached to those stones. Thinking, "I can't let that person go, they are counting on me," is a surefire sign that you may be giving beyond your means. Or, rather, that someone is asking you for too much.

Don't feel obligated to be generous in a certain way because you might let someone down. Remember, generosity at its core is how you see someone. What we do is an extension of that.

Generosity should lift up both the person who gives and the person who receives. If it isn't uplifting to both, then something is broken. It could be because the receiver is giving you gratitude stones you feel like you have to carry. Enabling someone in their dependent behavior is not being generous at all.

If you have not already given yourself permission to unpack those stones of gratitude and the obligatory generosity that comes along with them, then I give you permission to shed that unproductive weight right now!

Set Boundaries

After we have created a habit of saying yes to generosity in our lives, it's time to determine when to say no. This is a conversation I heard a novice winemaker retelling. To help illustrate that boundaries are in fact a good thing I want to share the story with you.

> Isaac, a new winemaker bought a vineyard and wanted to get into the wine business. A friend offered to mentor him. Isaac, the

owner of the vineyard, had done everything his mentor told him to do. After three years, he was excited when his grapes were growing and he could harvest them.

Well, his mentor understood how to make truly good wine. He wanted to teach Isaac to make the best wine possible. So, after three years of waiting for the vines to produce good mature grapes, the mentor told Isaac to cut half the fruit and drop it to the ground.

Isaac was devastated. He wanted to harvest all the grapes and make wine to maximize his vineyard and make the most wine possible. He wondered, why would he have to cut out half of his grapes he worked so hard to grow?

The vines are just like people. We have a finite amount of energy. So do the vines—if the vine's energy is spread too thin providing nutrients for too many grapes, then the quality of each grape will lessen.

To create the best wine, his mentor told him, you need to let the vines have the energy to give their best to what's there. Is the half you cut off good fruit? Yes! Here's the interesting part. By cutting off half of the grapes, you'd think that the wine would be twice as good. Not so. It's actually exponentially better!

Generosity is no different. We have areas of our lives where we can truly give our best self. The only way we can give our BEST self is to say no to things that are not in line with our priorities. This way, you can say yes to what you can give well within your interests and talents.

What do you need to say no to, so that what you say yes to becomes an exponentially better gift? That is a good question to ask on your generosity journey.

Acknowledge your sense to help, and then decide. We have so many things pulling at us. Job, relationships, safety, energy, skill sets. Sometimes saying no helps us to say yes to the right person or opportunity.

Think of it this way. I'm a terrible tailor, so saying yes to hem a dress for someone who desperately needs this service,is not putting my generosity to its highest potential. By saying no to that request or opportunity, I could say yes to something else I'm really good at and have time for, and that would be more impactful. And the person needing the dress hemmed could find someone who enjoys giving in that way and would therefore do a much better job.

Have the awareness that not only is it okay to say no, but when you say no, it's not because you don't want to. You are putting yourself in the place of highest potential. Other people will say yes to those opportunities because they'll fit their priorities and talents perfectly.

The Generosity Spectrum

As you start your Generosity Experiment, you'll notice that you, along with most, have particular attitudes toward generosity. Everyone's on a spectrum of taking and giving. Just as it's possible to take too much, it's also possible to give too much. It can take hard work, but you can break away from old habits to have a balanced, sustainable attitude toward generosity.

In his book *Givers and Takers,* Adam Grant lists four types of people that exist on the "generosity spectrum": Takers, Matchers, Self-Protective Givers, and Selfless Givers.[24]

1. **Takers**—They see every interaction to advance their own interests. They run rabid over a giver if you don't protect yourself. You will get better at spotting them over time. They act like they *deserve* your help and don't respect your time. They give you stones. Be sure to not carry those stones around.

2. **Matchers**—Trade for trade. They give as much as they get. They expect reciprocity. Transactional. Defensive stance. The result is less value for yourself and others. This attitude is effective when dealing with a taker. You do this for me, I do this for you. But this type of generosity is not heartfelt, and we will have trouble connecting with people.

3. **Self-Protective Givers (the sweet spot)**—They are generous but know their limits. They don't say yes to every single thing. They look for most impactful situations so they can sustain their generosity. It's not about sacrifice and tasking. You're not giving away

until you're destitute; it's about increasing your own happiness as you do it. It's like when you're on an airplane—put on your oxygen mask first before you help someone else with theirs, or you could pass out and be unhelpful to everyone else. This type will make sure they are protecting their ability to be generous.

4. **Selfless Givers**—These people have high concern for others and low concern for themselves. They set no boundaries. In short, these people burn out! They can usually be found stressed out and overburdened. They say yes to everybody; they are a magnet for takers. They exhaust themselves and then end up helping others less, falling short, doing everything halfway, etc. Their personal life suffers and they aren't doing the best job.

Always ask yourself, which fruit do I need to cut off in order to make this the best possible wine? It's all about balance. When you are evaluating your generosity, another powerful question to ask yourself is: "What can I say no to, so that what I say yes to will have an impact?"

Reactive Helping vs. Proactive Giving

Now that you realize that there should be balance in your generosity, you should also know that there are two approaches to giving.

1. **Reactive Helping**—You are asked to give.

2. **Proactive Giving**—You develop the idea to give.

When you are looking to fill your generosity bucket you have two methods you can use to add to it:

The first option, and the most-used option, is *reactive helping*. This method does not require much planning on your part. The majority of the opportunities you will have to fill up your generosity bucket reactively will be dictated to you based on both the habits you have created and whatever happens to be going on around you in each moment. Because you are not choosing these moments, there will be times that you feel stretched thin and lack the energy you need to fill your bucket.

The second method is called *proactive giving*. When using this method, before you put anything into the bucket, you will evaluate your priorities. Then you will be able to identify where you are most apt to be generous. Your deposits into the bucket will have the most impact if you can do things that will not only best serve others but you will enjoy doing.

If you choose this method, you will still have plenty of reactive helping opportunities, but as you practice proactive giving, you create a standard with which you say yes to opportunities to use your time and talents. This method allows you to fill up your bucket with both reactive helping and proactive giving, but you are the one in control. You are the one dictating how, when, and even who you will serve to fill your bucket.

Which method will you choose? The sad thing is that reactive helping is the default method when no choice has been made. When we fall into filling up our generosity bucket this way, we are not putting ourselves in a place to make the best choices for our lives. Proactive giving is really the only way to break out of our habit zone and step into the 10 percent.

Not all reactive helping is bad. The point is, as you start this journey, make sure to take a step back to see if it's the best thing for you. Are you going to act or be acted upon?

There was a national poll that took a look at what giving looked like for different demographics in the United States. The results were summarized into six profiles of giving:[24]

- Experts share knowledge.

- Coaches teach skills.

- Mentors give advice and guidance.

- Connectors make introductions.

- Extra-milers show up early, stay late.

- Helpers provide hands-on tasks, physical/financial support, and emotional support.

There are lots of ways to be generous. You don't have to fit into one of these categories. What makes sense to you? Don't try to be everything to everyone. Figure out what you can do well and do it. Start by saying yes to some opportunities and feeling out which ones felt good to you. Then you will be better equipped to zone in on what's best.

You've been given specific gifts and talents to share. It is our responsibility to develop and share those. When we choose what aligns with our priorities, generosity sustains itself. It fits into your life, but you're still pushing yourself to grow. Most importantly, it doesn't result in feeling burdened.

Let go of what you think generosity is "supposed" to be. Let go of what "type" of giver you think you should be. Let go of what you think others expect you to do or be.

Back in the introduction, we discussed the four stages of competence. Hopefully this book has helped you become fully aware of your old conventions and beliefs about generosity, and will assist you in consciously developing a Generosity Experiment that is right for you.

In summary, be sure to give while:

1. Keeping your priorities in line; say yes when it matters most.
2. Playing to your strengths.
3. Distributing the load more evenly (saying no sometimes).
4. Securing your oxygen mask first.
5. Amplifying impact for ways to help multiple people.

6. Learning to spot Takers. Steer clear when you need to. They will drain your energy. When you interact with them, develop a plan for how to manage them.

7. Identifying gratitude stones. Determine who is giving them to you, and how to set them down.

It may take some time to realize what type of generosity YOU are meant for. So go back through each chapter, take notes, and design your own Generosity Experiment. Develop that muscle, and you'll be amazed at how it changes you.

Chapter 9 Challenges:

- *For the next few days, make note of which giving opportunities leave you feeling drained, and which recharge you.*

- *Set boundaries so that you are giving in a way that is most impactful for you. Which "grapes" do you need to cut off so your generous actions can really shine?*

- *Identify the Takers in your life. How can you minimize their influence, so that you can keep giving in the "sweet spot"?*

Chapter 10
Starting YOUR Generosity Experiment

Real generosity in the future lies in giving all to the present. —Albert Camus, philosopher, journalist, and author

In this life we do the best we can to be happy and spread a little bit of that joy to the people around us. We do the best we can with the information and resources around. This process has helped me to be more intentional about the experience my life provides for me. It has made me more aware of the purpose in all my circumstances as well as made the lessons that they have to teach me more accessible.

What is generosity really? It is about truly seeing the other person and changing for the better as a result.

Because even though I may have more or less material possessions than another person, it doesn't mean my life is somehow better or worse. Sometimes people do need financial help, but what most need is someone to *see* them. And as I slowly learned this during my experiment, I began to change.

No matter what anyone tells you, ideas can and do change the world.. I think following through on the idea to embark on this Generosity Experiment was the best thing I ever did; it's certainly changed me, and I'm inviting you to change with me. The fruits of generosity are what we stay alive for.

From a line in a Walt Whitman poem "O Me! O Life!" his words echo a profound truth about our purpose in this life: "...the powerful play goes on, and you may contribute a verse." What will your verse be? What will you contribute to the world?

Lessons Learned

During my Generosity Experiment, the biggest hurdle I had to get past was my internal dialogue. Would it talk me out of helping if the situation was a little uncomfortable? If I let it, it would. Could I venture out of my comfort zone? I was determined to find out.

That is why I decided to start my Generosity Experiment. To focus on giving. To test whether I could be more generous. It was just twenty-one days of acting on every opportunity to be generous. Of saying yes when I would have normally said no.

I learned a lot in those twenty-one days. I realized that comparing myself to others, judging their circumstances against mine, in an effort to feel grateful and identify who was worthy of my generosity. I didn't have to do that—I could be grateful 100 percent of the time without comparing! After I realized that, the hard part was shutting up the part of my mind that automatically sought comparisons. That is why the intense focus of this experiment was so beneficial. It forced me to reckon with every knee-jerk responses I had.

My Generosity Experiment caused me to evaluate everything. I quickly found myself asking, *What is my true value system?*

And from there is where I get to start my new journey with new eyes aware of the majesty and beauty of this life . I couldn't believe how many opportunities there were to be generous that I hadn't noticed! I had been blind for far too long, and now I could finally see.

But then I had a new problem: it felt like there were so many opportunities, I couldn't keep up.

I couldn't give everything I had; I'd be exhausted. I had to choose MY version of being generous. So, how would I go about filtering through all the opportunities and deciding how and when to give?

The focused time during my Generosity Experiment allowed me to practice and figure out how to choose. At first, I wanted to give in the "right way" to the "right people," but over time I realized that was a flawed strategy—I was looking for what was expected of me rather than what felt right to me.

Part-way through my experiment, I threw that out the window and started over. I started to give without questioning. Even if it wasn't the "best" way to give according to conventional wisdom, I did it anyway.

Unfortunately, as much as I was improving, I could still only give with the information I had at the time, which was just my perspective. All I had were my own first impressions; I knew nothing about the very people I was trying to be generous to. How could I get another perspective?

By connecting.

This was one of the hardest parts of my Generosity Experiment. It's pretty easy to hand someone five dollars (use the person as a vehicle to feeling generous), but it's much harder to talk to them and get to know them a little. To see them as a person.

I began to attempt to connect with others, and it's then that I became vulnerable.

As you come to the last pages of this book, hopefully you've felt something. You've had an idea of something you could do—a way you could be generous. If you've felt a little nudge to be more generous (and ultimately make your life better), you must take IMMEDIATE action.

NOW!

Otherwise, nothing will change.

Cycle of Complacency

When you're on the verge of making an important decision or trying to change your perspective, the smartest thing to do is to do something that irrevocably commits you to the task—something that will make it difficult to not follow through. That is the difference between somebody who is merely going through the motions and somebody that is thriving and living abundantly.

For myself, the action that committed me to my Generosity Experiment was using social media as way to hold myself accountable. Then I invited others to do it with me.

Some of you have already decided that generosity could and should play a bigger part in your life. You have decided that you are not going to tolerate the status quo anymore, because you know that we won't get what we don't ask for.

The Dalai Lama was once asked, "What is the most important meditation we can do now?" Without batting an eye, he replied, "Critical thinking followed by action."

Discern what your world is, know the plot of the human drama, and then figure out where your talents might fit in to make a better world. Do something that makes your heart sing, and you will add to the chorus of life.

Life's too short to be ordinary. We get used to mediocrity until we realize we didn't want to live that way in the first place. It's time to STOP the cycle of complacency.

> *Give what you have. To someone, it may be better than you dare to think.*
> *—Henry Longfellow*

Generosity makes our world a better place. It improves the life of the receiver. And it improves the life of the giver. Yet, despite the benefits, real generosity is still too rare in our world today.

Instead, our culture has an insatiable desire for *more*. We look for happiness by focusing most of our resources toward our own pursuits: security, possessions, experiences, enjoyment, and luxury. Meanwhile, significant opportunities for generosity await us every day at every turn. In order to break out of the complacency cycle in a consumer-driven world and begin taking greater advantage of the abundant benefits of generosity, we need to shift our worldview.

What is to be gained from developing a more generous lifestyle?

You will realize the pie is big enough for everyone and not finite.

The scarcity mindset—that if my resources grow, someone else's must shrink—is based on a faulty premise. It assumes there is a finite-sized pie and that if someone else enjoys success, my opportunity shrinks. But this thinking is incorrect. The resource pie is not finite. It actually grows as people do well, as society benefits from others' success.

You will know that generosity leads to greater happiness.

Studies confirm what generous people already know: Giving increases happiness, fulfillment, and sense of purpose in the life of the giver.[25] We were not designed to be creatures of selfishness. Rather, we were designed to seek and discover happiness in loving and caring for others. And those who decide to look for fulfillment there quickly discover it.

You will find success in helping others succeed.

The easiest path to finding success in your life is to help someone else find theirs. After all, our contribution to this world has to be measured by something more significant than the size of our savings account. Our lives are going to achieve their greatest significance in how we choose to live them—and how we enable others to live theirs.

You will begin to believe changing even one life is worthwhile.

Generous people are quick to admit the world's problems will never be solved by one person…and, perhaps, never completely solved even years into the future. But trying to achieve perfection does not slow them. To them, changing even one life within their sphere of influence is reward enough. And it is a worthy endeavor to be sought.

Your trust in others will increase.

Generosity always requires trust. To invest individual resources into another person, we must believe, on some level, that they will be used to fill a purpose. Generous people are optimistic. And optimistic people are happy people because they choose to live in a world where belief in others is liberally employed.

You will be empowered to dream big dreams for your money.

Our money is only as valuable as what we choose to spend it on. Generous people use their excess to bring big dreams into reality. Our financial resources can be used to improve the quality of life for others. They can be used to make our communities safer, smarter, and more responsible. They can be used to make this world a little more pleasant for everyone. Indeed, generous people dream big dreams for their money, and so should we.

You see more resources to give than money.

We have so much more to offer this world than just financial resources. We have time, talents, experiences, and lessons learned. Generous people think beyond their money and begin to invest other aspects of their lives into others. Often, this step can be more difficult than signing a check, but usually, it is more desperately needed.

You can fully embrace the reality that life is short.

Life is short. And we only get one shot at it. Those who embrace this reality learn to live life in light of its brevity. They recognize we have limited time to leave our imprint on this world. And they cheerfully give their resources to accomplish it.

Our world is desperately seeking cheerful and generous givers. They improve society. They inspire us. They push us forward. And their view of the world is one I desire to further grow in my own life.

YOUR 21 Day Generosity Experiment

I invite you to begin your own Generosity Experiment. Put it on the calendar and start today.

For me, my experiment was launched with a simple question: How can I be more generous?

No matter your starting point, a Generosity Experiment is just twenty-one days of focusing on giving. That's it! It's a pretty simple concept. But then comes the hard part: putting yourself out there and giving with abandon.

The beauty of developing your own Generosity Experiment is that YOU get to decide how to do it. You get to decide how you will be generous.

I could tell you exactly what to do step-by-step, but how effective would that be? You decide the rules, parameters, methods. Hopefully this book has given you insight into ideas of what you could incorporate.

Why twenty-one days? Deliberately focusing on generosity every day, for three full weeks will help you unlock a higher level of living, it will increase your generosity output into the world, and ultimately, will change you.

Spend twenty-one days saying yes. Of course, saying no is sometimes vital, but as you start your own experiment, develop a habit of going out of your comfort zone. Are you saying no simply because you're scared? Then give anyway. You'll be helping someone who may have otherwise been passed by, and in the process, you will change and realize what you were meant to do.

There are so many blessings generosity can bring to your relationships, perspective, job, family, etc. As you change, you will see everything differently.

How will your Generosity Experiment look? Come up with your own hypothesis. Although you come up with it and choose how to carry it out, there will be many that get to benefit from the results of it.

Raise the level of your life. Break the chains of living in your habit zone.

Has this book inspired you to ask questions about yourself and your life? Are you living the life you want to live? Could you be happier and more connected?

If you were intrigued reading this book, prove it. Don't just put it down and move on with your life. I invite you to try this experiment to see if this is true. Start your own Generosity Experiment today. Don't wait!

For resources and ideas, check out my website www.thegenerosityexperiment.com, which has a link to a Facebook group of others starting their experiments. You can also find links to podcasts on different aspects of generosity.

We can work together and support each other in this. Make a video explaining your experiences and what you've learned, and share it with us.

Let's start a revolution. A generosity revolution.

Chapter 10 Challenges:

- *Start your own Generosity Experiment!*
- *Visit TheGenerosityexperiment.com website for ideas. Listen to a podcast. Watch a video.*
- *Finally, let generosity catch on in your life, and watch as it catches on around you.*

Conclusion

My hope and prayer is that *Redefining Generosity* has helped you reflect on your life and evaluate your participation in being a proactive force of generosity, more deeply than you ever could have on your own.

I hope this process has proven valuable to you. However, there is one more thing I need to tell you: You are not finished. In fact, you have just begun. You may have started applying some of the concepts and principles in this book already as you were reading, and though your general course may be set, you should not expect your vision of what generosity should look like to stay static. As you learn, grow, and experiment, your understanding will deepen and your purpose will be magnified.

As you continue to deepen your connection and compassion for others, don't forget to apply those lessons to how you view yourself.

Keep this book close by use it with your family, colleagues, and friends.

May God bless you and may you be a source of gratitude in the lives of others.

About the Author

Jayson Linford is a passionate Self-help Author and Serial Entrepreneur on a lifelong mission to help people dismantle that "no outlet" sign in their lives, so they can step into their best version and actualize their dreams. After countless trials and triumphs (including overcoming bankruptcy, owning multiple businesses, and being a stay-at-home dad), he has acquired invaluable wisdom that he strives to share with others for their greater good.

Most recently, Jayson conducted a generosity experiment, spending time redefining both his habits and mindset toward generosity. *Redefining Generosity* documents his entire transformative journey.

When he isn't inspiring others through the power of words, Jayson enjoys coaching and cycling. He is also an avid fitness enthusiast. However, his number one priority is and will always be his amazing family.

To find out more about Jayson Linford, feel free to visit his official website at www.jaysonlinford.com

START YOUR OWN EXPERIMENT

You are invited…..

If this book has prompted you to start your own generosity experiment then let me be the first to say... GO FOR IT!

To assist you in making your generosity experiment the best it can possibly be I have assembled some tools for you to use if you wish at:

TheGenerosityExperiment.com

One of my favorite quotes is…

> "The dark does not destroy the light; it defines it. It's our fear of the dark that casts our joy into the shadows."
> Brené Brown

Sometimes the dark can feel overwhelming, but it is also an opportunity to be defined. Light never retreats. When you crack a door into a dark room it is always the light that pierces the dark. This experiment allowed me to be that light pushing back the darkness and my hope is that it creates the same defining moments in your life.

Endnotes

1. A.H. Maslow,. "A Theory of Human Motivation," *Psychological Review* 50, no. 4 (1943): 370-96, doi:10.1037/h0054346

2. Corrie Ten Boom and Elizabeth Sherrill, The Hiding Place, 2015 Hendrickson Publishers, pp 206-210.

3. Keith Mano, "How a 20th century eye operation shows the Bethsaida miracle actually happened," *Hoshuha.com*, http://www.hoshuha.com/resources/bethsaida.html

4. Maxwell Maltz, *Psycho-Cybernetics* ,108 (New Jersey: Prentice Hall Press, 1960).

5. David McRaney, You can beat your brain: how to turn your enemies into friends, how to make better decisions, and other ways to be less dumb,60 (New York: Oneworld, 2013.)

6. Published March 27, 2001 by Bartleby.com; © 2001 Copyright Bartleby.com, Inc.

7. James Herring and James Barton Longacre, *National portrait gallery of distinguished americans*, Volume 2 (South Carolina: Nabu Press, 2012), 15.

8. Lindsay Murdoch, "'Poverty Porn'; Charity body denounces use of 'pity' advertising in fundraising campaigns," *The Sydney Morning Herald*, June 7, 2016, http://www.smh.com.au/world/lindsay-20160607-gpdeec.html.

9. Ash Beckham, *We're All Hiding Something. Let's Find the Courage to Open Up*, video, TEDx, 9:22, September 2013, https://www.ted.com/talks/ash_beckham_we_re_all_hiding_something_let_s_find_the_courage_to_open_up

10. Bob Burg and John David Mann, *The Go-Giver*, (London: Portfolio, 2007).

11. John Joseph Powell, *The Secret of Staying in Love* (Argus Communications, 1974).

12. *The Bridge*, directed by Eric Steele (2006; New York City; IFC Films), Documentary Film.

13. Eknath Easwaran and Michael N. Nagler, *The Upanishads* (Petaluma, CA: Nilgiri Press),1987.

14. Stephen R. Covey, *7 Habits of Highly Effective People 25th anniversary edition* (New York: RosettaBooks), 2013.

15. Og Mandino, *The Greatest Salesman in the World* (New York: Random House, 2011).

16. Charles Darwin, *The Descent of Man*, (CreateSpace Independent Publishing Platform, 2014)?

17. Darwin's assertions have been borne out by K.R. Munroe's 1996 study of individuals who risked

their own lives to rescue strangers, *The Heart of Altruism: Perceptions of A Common Humanity*.

18. Angela A. Stanton and Sheila Ahmadi, "Oxytocin Increases Generosity in Humans," *PLOS ONE* 2, no. 11 (2007): https://doi.org/10.1371/journal.pone.0001128"

19. Abigail Marsh, "Why some poeple are more altruistic than others," TEDSummit, video, 12:21, June 2016, https://www.ted.com/talks/abigail_marsh_why_some_people_are_more_altruistic_than_others

20. "Humans are hardwired for connection? Neurobiology 101 for parents, educators, practioners, and the general public," *Wellesly Centers for Women, September 15, 2010,* https://www.wcwonline.org/2010/humans-are-hardwired-for-connection-neurobiolo

21. Jonathan Haidt, "Elevation and the positive psychology of morality," in Flourishing: Positive psychology and the life well-lived, ed. C.L.M. Keyes and J. Haidt (Washington D.C.: American Psychological Association, 2003), 275–289.

22. Robert A. Heinlein, *Between Planets* (London: Robert Hale Ltd, 2002), .

23. Linda Holmes, "'Missing Richard Simmons' And The Nature Of Being Known," *NPR.org*, March 21, 2017. http://www.npr.org/sections/monkeysee/2017/03/21/520943717/missing-richard-simmons-and-the-nature-of-being-known

24. Adam Grant, *Give and Take: Why Helping Others Drives Our Success* (New York: Penguin Books, 2014).

25. Carolyn Gregoire, "The Giving Habits of Americans May Surprise You (INFOGRAPHIC)," *Huffpost*, August 20, 2013: http://www.huffingtonpost.com/2013/08/20/are-you-a-giver-huffpost-_n_3785215.html

www.ingramcontent.com/pod-product-compliance
Lightning Source LLC
Chambersburg PA
CBHW051648040426
42446CB00009B/1033